THE
RAILWAY AGE

THE
RAILWAY AGE

Michael Robbins

MANDOLIN

First published 1962 by Routledge & Kegan Paul

Published 1965 by Penguin Books

This edition published 1998 by
Mandolin, an imprint of Manchester University Press,
Oxford Road, Manchester MI3 9NR, UK
and Room 400, 175 Fifth Avenue, New York, NY 10010, USA

Distributed exclusively in the USA by
St. Martin's Press, Inc., 175 Fifth Avenue, New York,
NY 10010, USA

Distributed exclusively in Canada by
UBC Press, University of British Columbia, 6344 Memorial Road,
Vancouver, BC, Canada V6S 1Z2

British Library Cataloguing-in-Publication Data
A catalogue record for this book is available from the British Library

Library of Congress Cataloging-in-Publication Data
Robbins, Michael.
    The railway age / Michael Robbins.
       p. cm.
    ISBN 1-901341-09-7
     1. Railroads—Great Britain—History. 2. Railroads—History.
  I. Title
  HE3018.R55   1998
  385'.0941—dc21   98-2901

ISBN 1 901341 09 7 *paperback*

Third edition published 1998

05 04 03 02 01 00 99 98   10 9 8 7 6 5 4 3 2 1

Typeset in Adobe Garamond
by Koinonia Limited, Manchester

Printed in Great Britain
by Clays Ltd, St Ives Plc

Contents

Preface

This is not a history of railways. It is a longish essay about various aspects of the history of railways and the effects they have had on the world around them. It is mostly about railways and society in nineteenth-century Britain, with a rapid sketch of development in other countries.

I have chosen to write it in this way, and at this length, because I hope that it may attract the notice of two different sorts of people who are not likely to tolerate a long book: first, historians or teachers of history, who sometimes overlook when they are writing or teaching about the nineteenth century that social life and politics were revolutionized by the railway during that period; and second, men and women in my own profession of transport, who ought to be more aware than they are of the historical background to their activities. Neither sort of person will find anything here that is entirely novel, either among the facts stated or the reflections I make on them; but I have tried to assemble and set them out in a way which is, as far as I know, fresh. If my two presumed readers will have the patience to read through to the end of the essay, I think that they will at any rate have found something to argue about.

Because it is this kind of book, I have not interrupted the text or burdened the page with footnotes; but because every reader is entitled if he wishes to know what evidence is being called, I have set out my authorities relating to each chapter in a manner which makes it possible and not unduly difficult for everyone who really wants to follow up a reference to do so.

The typescript of this book has been read by three friends: D. S. M. Barrie, Charles E. Lee, and Jack Simmons, and their help has enabled me to correct and improve it greatly.

But none of them agrees with every opinion or judgement that is expressed. On particular points I have had valuable assistance from the Archivist (Historical Records) of the British Transport Commission. My wife, Elspeth Robbins, helped me greatly in making the index and in other ways that every author's wife will know.

Michael Robbins
(1962)

Preface to the 1998 edition

For the reissue of this book, thirty-six years after its original publication, I thought it best to make only a limited number of alternations to the text. Some corrections of factual statements have been made, and at a few places account has been taken of work published which bears directly on relevant matters, which I should have referred to if I had known of it at the time I wrote. But essentially this is a republication of what may be seen as a 'period piece', without subsequent revision based on hindsight.

The Notes on sources have, however, been somewhat expanded, principally in order to direct the reader who wishes to delve further into significant works published since the 1960s. This is not meant to be a comprehensive bibliography, but a pointer to certain major contributions to the history of the high railway age. The Postscript offers a few reflections on the railway and transport scene in Britain as it now appears to me.

Michael Robbins

Chapter 1

What is a railway?

The railway age! The term has often been used: sometimes, by English writers, as a rough equivalent to the Victorian age; sometimes, by Americans, to indicate the great era of expansion after 1865 and the final triumphant settlement of the West. It is not a precise term; some people may think it a tendentious label. To attach the label to a historical period needs justification. To begin with it simply provokes questions. Was there really in any significant sense a railway age? If there was, when did it begin? Who was responsible for creating it? Has it left any permanent and recognizable mark on the landscape? Has human society been affected by it? Have politics and the map of the world been changed because of it? Is there something about the railway that made it characteristic of an age and significant above, or along with, other influences at work in its day? Are we still living in a railway age, or has it ended?

Short and comparatively simple answers might be given to these questions. They could be dealt with like this: There was a railway age. It began with the Liverpool & Manchester Railway in 1830 and lasted until the First World War. If responsibility for it is to be assigned to one man, that man was George Stephenson. The age has left its mark on the physical landscape, on social organization, on political groupings, and on the map of the world. The railway, with its allies the electric telegraph and the steamship, virtually annihilated distance and became, at one bound, the most potent physical influence on the development of the world in the nineteenth century. Since the First World War, the railway age has developed into something much more complex.

But short and simple answers like this will hardly do. The questions should have been more artfully put, and very much more prudently answered. There is, to start with, doubt and ambiguity about the very term 'railway'. Who is quite certain what a railway is? Everyone, of course, feels perfectly sure that he knows a railway when he sees it. But, like all well-known, commonplace things, it is remarkably difficult to define neatly. Taken solely in its mechanical aspect, the railway is a device for moving vehicles which are provided with wheels of a special pattern upon parallel rails along a prepared track. This is adequate so far as it goes, and of course it contains the element which is fundamental to the railway; but it is equally applicable to a street tramway, or to a private railway within a works, or to a cable-operated line along a seaside pier. It is not full enough to define the railway, that complex instrument that created an age of its own and changed the course of events.

The definition which seems to come nearest to comprehending the railway as we know it, with its different necessary attributes, is one put forward by Mr Charles E. Lee, as follows: 'Broadly, the modern railway may be regarded as a combination of four main features, namely: (a) specialized track; (b) accommodation of public traffic; (c) conveyance of passengers; and (d) mechanical traction.'

To Mr Lee's list, however, we must add one more feature of another kind to make the specification complete: '(e) some measure of public control.'

This list, as extended, presents a mixture of technical, economic, and political elements. All five features have to be present together before there is a railway; when one or more of them is absent, then there is a tramway, or a light railway, or a private means of transport, or something else. These five necessary conditions of the railway must be examined in turn.

'Specialized track' is rightly placed first. It is the fundamental mechanical condition of the whole thing. It is a wonderfully simple device; but, far from bursting on the world in a moment of glorious revelation, it had to undergo a long-drawn-out development, and in Britain it set off at one time on a course that proved to be abortive. Satisfactory materials were not to be had when railway track was first devised; development and invention of new techniques went on for nearly two centuries before requirements were adequately met.

'Specialized track' here means two things: a specially-formed track consisting of parallel rails which can be used only by vehicles having wheels of appropriate shape at the right distance apart; and sole and complete occupation of the land on which the track is laid. The requirement for the rails is that they should present a continuous flat surface on which the flat tread of the vehicle wheels can run, with convenient facility for making junctions (by means of points, switches, or turn-outs, terms which mean the same thing) and for crossing ordinary highways on the level without undue interference with their surface. Correspondingly, the wheels must include a flange, or extended rim, somewhere on the tread section, to hold them to the rails and prevent the vehicle from moving laterally off them. In practice, a flange at the inner edge of the wheels has been found most convenient and is now universally employed.

Another possibility had, however, to be tried and discarded; this was to restrain the sideways movement of vehicles by a raised lip or flange on the track itself. This development was known as the 'plateway'; its name still survives in Britain in the word 'platelayer', meaning the man who lays and maintains railway permanent way. But the railway was destined to develop with the edge-rail; and as iron rails designed to carry vehicles on their top sides were manufactured with increasing success, the plateway was seen to be a blind alley.

The words 'specialized track' also cover the sole and complete occupation of the land on which the track is laid. If this condition is not fulfilled, the undertaking is not a railway but a works or street tramway, sharing the ground it runs on with other kinds of user. That is the essential difference between railways and tramways. The distinction has always been clear in Britain, and in Europe generally; only at a very few places, and in unusual circumstances like the approaches to docks (at Weymouth, for example), does the railway train emerge on to the street, where with special precautions the general traffic is prevented from colliding with railway vehicles. In America, however, the distinction has not always been so clear, and the main city streets of Syracuse, N.Y., were traversed for one and a half miles by the main line of the New York Central Railroad until a new alignment, with tracks segregated from the streets, was built in 1936. Only a short time before, a similar operation had to be carried out at London, Ontario. American conditions were of course different from those in Europe; the railroad has often arrived before the town. But in England the 'Parliamentary fence' along the tracks, which the railway had to maintain under statute, is as old as the main lines of railway themselves. Later on, some lines of track were allowed to be built alongside highways without segregation, either for economy or for more convenient handling of short-distance local traffic; the Wantage Tramway of 1875 and the Welshpool & Llanfair Light Railway of 1903 are examples. These were clearly not the same as railways, pure and simple; their very names indicate that a distinction was felt and understood. In 1868 Parliament had acknowledged the 'light railway' as something that might be considerably more specialized than a street tramway and yet still fall short of being a railway. Though there are hybrids – tramways which use 'reserved tracks' at some parts of their routes, and railways which traverse public roads and streets here and there – yet there is rarely much doubt about which side of the line any particular specimen falls on. Specialized track, in both senses, special shape and sole user, is the essence of the railway.

'Accommodation of public traffic' is the second requisite. This requires less comment. So long as the line of rails with its associated wagons, however ingenious or economical it may be as a device for haulage, is run purely as an adjunct to the proprietor's main business, say of mining or quarrying, it can have little impact on the general economy. Such a line is not faced with the great problems that the railway as public haulier has to contend with – safety; rates and charges for traffic; accountability to the public. There are still private wagonways and tramroads, mostly in mining districts, used for conveyance of workmen; but if they do not accommodate public traffic, they remain subsidiary parts of a production process, not railways in their own right.

'Conveyance of passengers' may at first sight seem a strange partner in this list; but it is in fact an essential condition. Acceptance of passenger traffic, and the consequent responsibility for safe working of trains, force the railway management to adopt a code of practices which is significantly different from that which is held to be sufficient when inanimate freight only is involved. So the internal working of the railway is much affected by the decision to offer conveyance to passengers; even more important is the external effect on the district which it traverses. It is a curious feature of the early railway age in England that, although the railways were promoted primarily with a view to haulage of freight traffic, passengers being in most cases considered of secondary importance, the original expectations were reversed: passenger traffic astonished the early managements by its volume, and the total receipts from passengers remained greater than those from freight throughout the whole of the first two main-line railway decades. Only after 1850 did the slower-moving processes of industrial and commercial change in Britain catch up with the personal decisions of individuals, and in 1852 for the first time the revenue produced by charges levied for freight transport exceeded the total of fares paid by passengers. The significant thing about this is the immense unsatisfied demand for passenger travel that must have been awaiting the arrival of railways. In some parts of England stage coaches offered frequent services, as was the case in the West Riding, for example; but each coach could carry only eleven passengers, which meant that not more than some 180 passengers a day could travel each way between Leeds and Bradford by public transport before the railway came. This was less than half a single train load. The average number of passengers carried weekly by the Leeds & Selby Railway during the summer of 1835 was 3,500 against 400 previously by the coaches on the same route. Regular and safe communication had been offered in most places by coaches, but not in adequate volume, or at a satisfactory fare. The augmented volume and the cheapness of passenger conveyance that the railways provided was one of their most important distinguishing features in relation to the world they lived in; it was something that was not paralleled until the arrival of the internal-combustion engine and its application to transport on the road.

'Mechanical traction' is equally necessary. It imports the element of speed. It was the speed of the railway that smashed the coaches on the trunk routes and most of the canals. The other features of the railway already mentioned might have produced many minor and local advantages; but it was the element of speed, based on mechanical traction, which meant that the railway could knock the nineteenth century sideways. Speed for personal transit; speed in delivering mails and newspapers; speed for milk and perishable foodstuffs; speed in moving troops – these were the things that the locomotive engine presented to the railway at once. Later, when in the course of development three men, two on the locomotive in front and one on the brake van at the rear, with the aid of course of other men in signal boxes and about the tracks, could move 1,000 tons or more of coal over great distances, then technical efficiency was allied to speed. The combination was, in its time, nearly irresistible (though the railway in England never put the coastal collier out of business). Speed of operation was the root of the efficiency which was reflected in low fares and charges for freight; and cheap transport had effects that ran through the whole of economic and social life.

The last feature in the list is 'some measure of public control'. It became clear very early that the railway would be immensely important to the life of the community it served, and the public authorities everywhere were quick to organize measures of public control. There were different conceptions in different countries about how far it was right for the state to organize or regulate commercial undertakings, including those with such a great impact on the national life as the railway was obviously going to have: Britain, France, Belgium, Prussia and the United States all began with different notions. Most of the measures of public control that were adopted were onerous, because the community was afraid of the railway. No branch of the economy was so clearly linked to the effective exercise of political authority and military power. As the nineteenth century went on, controls by the public authorities tended to grow more intensive, both in the matter of rates and charges and in regard to safety of working; and later on in questions of railway employment also. It would be a mockery to label the British Parliament's frequent nineteenth-century interventions in the railway business as a 'policy'; but if there is any trend to be discerned amid the fluctuations of action, it is towards closer control by state-created agencies. The same is true in the United States, where the Interstate Commerce Commission legislation of 1887 clamped a degree of control on the railroads which was in some respects tighter than anything known by the private companies in Britain. On the continent of Europe, *étatisme* in relation to railways began as soon as the first railways were projected; given the political atmosphere of those countries, it was the natural thing to happen; but state ownership and management, as opposed to state control, were not accepted automatically or continuously pursued. The relation of the railways and the state is a chequered story – indeed, the American Charles Francis Adams, writing in 1876, called it *the* railway problem; and the last chapter has not been written yet.

Chapter 2

Forerunners and pioneers

The railway was a child of the English North-East. It first appeared quite grown up in the North-West; but wagonways of a humble sort had been in use in and about the lower valley of the River Tyne for something like 150 years before the Liverpool merchants in the eighteen-twenties staked large parts of their fortunes on rails and flanged wheels. Wagonways on which chaldrons of coal were hauled by horses from coal-pits down to the loading staiths on the Tyne and Wear were a familiar feature of the Northumberland and Durham landscape before 1700, and by 1810, when George Stephenson of North Wylam, ten miles west of Newcastle, went to work on the steam engines at Killingworth pit, eight miles north, there was a spidery network of railways stretching back into the country from each side of the two rivers. These were private installations, mere adjuncts to the business of getting and marketing coal, worked with very little aid from mechanical power; but on them several generations of engineers had tackled the basic problems of the track, points and crossings, and minor constructional work. Not always minor: the Tanfield wagonway required a handsome stone-arched bridge to carry it over a valley, and there was a long tunnel built about 1770, virtually an underground railway, on the East Kenton line.

The archaeology of railways can take the researcher into some queer places: into the streets of ancient Syracuse, if he will, to find artificial ruts in the stone paving about four feet apart, or to Malta, or even to the Propylaea of the Acropolis of Athens. The earliest known representation of a wagon running on rails (with outside flanges) is a glass image on the so-called Rappoltsteiner cup, now in Munich, which relates to Ste. Marie-aux-Mines in Alsace and is dated 1543. A treatise called *De Re Metallica*, by a German whose name was latinized as Agricola, printed at Basle in 1556, contained a woodcut showing a little cart standing on a wooden track at the opening of a surface mine-working; it is guided by a blunt iron pin or prong running in the narrow gap left between the rails. The first written mention of a railway in Britain so far discovered is in the manuscript accounts of Sir Francis Willoughby's estates at Wollaton Hall, near Nottingham; this line is probably to be dated 1603–4. Legal proceedings are evidence for a railway existing at Broseley in Shropshire in 1605, and there were others in the same county in the Coalbrookdale area and at Kinlet on the Staffordshire border, and one possibly at Inveresk near Edinburgh, all before 1660.

During the eighteenth century, a fundamental divergence of practice in an important technical respect took place which has caused much bother to later investigators and historians. This was the point: either the flanges, which were essential to prevent the vehicle moving sideways off the rails, could be on the wheels themselves (the original practice), or they could be on the rails. In the former case the rails ('edge-rails') held up the vehicle, which did not, or was not supposed to, touch the ground; in the latter ('plate-rails', made of iron angles laid end to end), the wheels of the vehicle were flat and rested directly on the web of the iron plate. The second method had the advantage that it did not require a special type of wheels on the vehicle, only that their distance apart should fit the plates. The same wagons could thus use roads and plateways. The original method eventually prevailed (partly because of the difficulty of making a workable switch, or pair of points, for plate rails), but before it did so many plateways were constructed, mostly between 1795 and 1815. A late example of a public plateway surviving in use (though not in regular use) was the Ticknall Tramroad in Leicestershire on which a horse pulled a wagon to maintain the right of way annually until 1917.

After the North-East, South Wales (with Monmouthshire) the home of many early railways. In that mountainous countryside, canals could at best be of limited usefulness, and plateways, mostly short, connected the pits with the nearest navigable water. All these western lines were of the Shropshire type, with smaller wagons and a track gauge no more than 3ft. 9in. There were also isolated outlying railways in some distant parts of Britain. In Scotland, a wagonway traversed the battlefield of Prestonpans in 1745 – it had been there since 1722, carrying coal down from the pits at Tranent to a quay at Cockenzie; and there were lines on the north side of the Forth, at the Carron company's ironworks near Falkirk, and in Lanarkshire and Ayrshire. The first railway for which an Act of Parliament was passed was Charles Brandling's Middleton colliery line, close to Leeds, of 1758. The Forest of Dean was early riddled with tramways; the Surrey Iron Railway, from Croydon to Wandsworth, was authorized in 1801, the first railway in the London district and the first railway promoted independently of a canal to be sanctioned by Parliament; two horsed tramways were pursuing their wiggly courses over Dartmoor by 1820; a railway twenty-four miles long was opened in 1818 from Brecon to the remote Herefordshire village of Eardisley; and in the same year Sir Walter Scott and other lairds were busy promoting a line up the valley of the Gala Water and down to Edinburgh.

These were all railways acting, as it were, on their own; but many canals used short lines of railway as feeders. The Grand Junction Canal had a railway line from Blisworth to Northampton, later replaced by a canal branch, and it used a railway as a temporary link while the tunnel from Blisworth to Stoke Bruerne was being constructed. In the north, the Lancaster Canal, running up to Kendal, had an intermediate railway link near Preston where the ground was not favourable to canal levels. On the other hand, the Canterbury & Whitstable was planned throughout as a railway, tunnel and all, and it was opened in May 1830 with a locomotive (for passenger trains) and most of the outward marks of the fully-developed railway; it introduced season tickets in 1834. The most illustrious predecessor of the Liverpool & Manchester was, however, the Stockton & Darlington of 1825.

This famous line has often been saluted as the first true railway, and its construction and opening were notable events; but by the tests we are now applying it just fails to qualify. Locomotive traction was certainly employed from the start, but horses did some of the work, and all the passenger part of the business was done by a contractor using horsed coaches. The Stockton & Darlington marked a great step forward in the organization of the railway: it brought together into one organism several of its principal features, and its use of locomotives for public freight traffic was momentous. Yet it was the curtain-raiser, not the first act. The Liverpool & Manchester directors had still to take many decisions on matters of principle before their line was opened: the two most important were not to employ contractors for the conveyance of traffic on their railway but to handle all the business directly, and to use steam haulage for all traffic. Once these were decided, and put into effect, the drama of the railway had begun.

The five features of the railway as we know it are therefore found, separately and in various combinations, appearing at different times and places from the sixteenth century until the nineteenth; but it was not until the Liverpool & Manchester Railway was formally opened by the Duke of Wellington on Wednesday, 15 September 1830, that the Railway, a public carrier of passengers and freight on rail by mechanical traction under statutory authority, stood plain for all to see.

It was a memorable occasion: on its own account, for the importance of the event, which brought out some 50,000 people to witness it at Liverpool alone; for the fatal accident to William Huskisson, former President of the Board of Trade and Colonial Secretary, a leader of the Liverpool men who were behind the new railway; for the strained political atmosphere which caused the Manchester police super-intendent to advise the Duke to leave the town, by railway, as quickly as possible after his arrival; and also for the profound but erroneous impression that it made upon the young poet Tennyson, who was present there and thought the wheels ran in grooves on the rails. That was why he wrote afterwards (in *Locksley Hall*) about the 'ringing grooves of change'. He was wrong about the 'grooves'; he was really meaning railways, not tram-lines.

The Liverpool & Manchester was the place, and the year 1830 the date, of the birth of the railway age. Then the railway stood forth as a portent, and it made men think very hard, if not always very sensibly; for, in combining these different characteristics for the first time, it became something different in kind, not merely in degree, from the earlier forms of inland transport by road and water. It was, to look at, merely a technical device – or rather an assembly of various independent inventions in civil and mechanical engineering. But even in 1830 a man with prescience could see farther than that. What might he have foreseen as he looked that September afternoon at the processions of carriages and wagons, laden with an immense company of people, which were dragged by labouring steam engines across the level plain of south Lancashire? With the advantage of hindsight, we may answer for him; but there is no reason why he should not have discerned something like this.

By the standards of the day, and for many years to come, the railway would virtually annihilate the effects of distance for the traveller. It would reduce the duration and the cost of transport for goods, so that the manufacturer could almost at once begin to ignore the distance that his products had to be hauled over land as a serious element in the cost of manufacturing and selling. The railway would link distant places, and so strengthen the hand of central authority and weaken provincial loyalties. It would make labour more mobile, able to pursue work from place to place, not merely in long-term, or regular seasonal, movements of migration but from month to month. Allied with the telegraph and the newspaper, it would convey opinions as well as persons and freight, and thus transform national and international political life by linking the fringes more closely with the centre. In addition, it would make it possible for an enormous number of people to travel, not with any economic intention or immediate significance, but just for travel's own sake, for pleasure. It would stimulate production, and make distribution speedy. It would require coal, and iron, and machine products, in immense quantities, both directly for itself and at one remove for the industries that its existence would promote or make possible. It would call for an army of men to work it: labourers, artisans, clerks, engineers, and managers. It would require great financial outlay, and new forms and techniques of administration. And those who controlled this army and this machine would wield great power.

Chapter 3

George Stephenson and the great builders

The railway pioneers were a notable body of men. Most of them began life with few advantages, apart from a copious endowment of character. Almost all of them, apart from I. K. Brunel of the Great Western, came from modest, if not actually humble, origins, and their biographers, headed by the unlovable Samuel Smiles, were at pains to demonstrate them as shining examples of 'Self-Help'. Unfortunately, that is a virtue that has upon the whole failed to commend itself to succeeding generations as being at all attractive, and the impression left on the minds of most people who think of them at all is that the great originators of the railways must have been a dull and priggish lot. This is a pity, because they were in fact men of high quality, whose talents would command respect at any time and in any company.

George Stephenson has been called the father of railways; and that judgement stands the test of challenge. He was not the inventor of railways – no one man was that; but George Stephenson, with encouragement and invaluable support from other men, himself established the railway, as an organism in the sense we have already defined. He made the thing work.

Samuel Smiles asserted this so forthrightly in the first edition of his celebrated biography, published in 1857, that a great hubbub ensued. Sharp rejoinders were put out, in which anticipations by other men of this or that feature which the Stephensons adopted or perfected were demonstrated. In later editions, Smiles withdrew or modified some of his claims for Stephenson, and to that extent his critics were successful. But the disputants missed the point. The steam locomotive on rails had been devised by Richard Trevithick and first put to work on the Penydarren tramroad, near Merthyr Tydfil in South Wales, in 1804, at least eight years before George Stephenson turned his mind actively to the steam locomotive; Matthew Murray of Leeds and William Hedley and Timothy Hackworth of Wylam, on Tyneside, were developing some of its most important features before, or at the same time as, Stephenson's work; William James and Thomas Gray had visions of far-reaching, even national, networks of railways before 1830. But no number of such mere chronological anticipations can shake the significance of Stephenson's achievement. He brought the railway, as a working, living organism, into being.

There would have been much less misunderstanding about the nature of Stephenson's work if people had not persisted in regarding it as principally a matter of mechanical engineering. The invention of the steam locomotive has tended to steal the picture. In its development, though Stephenson certainly played a very prominent part, he has to share the credit with a number of other men. But he has more important claims. Together with his equally gifted son Robert, he was really more notable as a civil engineer – the actual construction of the Liverpool & Manchester Railway was a prodigious feat for its age, and it was immediately recognized as such. But he was outstanding as the organizer of success. His administrative methods may have been undeveloped, but he had a conception, shared by some of his influential backers in the eighteen-twenties but not at that time by the professional engineers, of the railway as an entity – of its construction, motive power, commercial potentialities, and internal management – underlying all his immense activity. What was more important, he had the force of character to convince doubters and to override obstinate opposition. This is well shown in the minutes of evidence on the first Liverpool & Manchester Railway bill, which have been reprinted and are not difficult to come by. They show the best legal brains of the capital set against the self-educated mechanic from Tyneside; and they show how character at length got the victory over brains. Not that Stephenson was destitute of brains – far from it; but it was tenacity of character that secured victory for the bill, at the second attempt. Stephenson showed during the hearings on the first bill that he had the stuff in him that would command eventual success; and it did.

The task that confronted him was staggering. He had to plan and oversee the execution, as a speculative commercial undertaking, of an enormous task: the construction of thirty-one miles of double railway through difficult country, involving a steep climb in tunnel at the Liverpool end, several awkward bridges and viaducts, and a section over the notorious bog of Chat Moss that nobody quite knew how to deal with. He had to collect and manage the labour force; he had to order and inspect supplies of materials in unprecedented quantities; he had to do all these things at a time when business enterprise was still confined almost absolutely to the single master, when factories or mills might employ up to 200 hands. Thomas Telford had dealt with problems of a similar kind, though smaller in volume and complexity, on the Caledonian Canal of 1804–22. But perhaps only the Royal Navy afforded a parallel in those days to the complex organization that had to be created for the Liverpool & Manchester Railway; and those responsible for the Navy were not staking their future upon barely-tried technical innovations.

While all this was going forward in Lancashire, Stephenson somehow found time to devote thought to other railway projects. In 1829 his influence was certainly the reason for the decision of the Leicester & Swannington Railway directors to use the same gauge as the Stockton & Darlington, the Liverpool & Manchester, and the Canterbury & Whitstable. How much the Australians, with three different main-line gauges in their continent, must wish that they had had a Stephenson to convince them! He had found 4ft. 8in. on the Killingworth wagonway and used it on the early railways he built – the Stockton & Darlington retained this dimension until 1840, when, for reasons still obscure, another half-inch was added (which did not mean any alteration to the rolling-stock). Other steam railways of the early period varied between 4ft. 8in. and 4ft. 9in. for many years.

The facts of Stephenson's life are on record, and it is not likely that there is much to add to what is already known about them. But there must be a good many of his letters about which have not been published, and they would certainly deepen our impression of him. One such has recently been printed, from the Hulton manuscripts in the Lancashire Record Office at Preston. It was written to the committee of the Bolton & Leigh Railway, while that line was being planned.

Liverpool Nov 14th, 1824

Gentlemen

Having duly considered the various Lines of the intended Road proposed to Mr Steel and having the Sections of two before me the practicability of the one and the impracticability of the other is so obvious it is unnecessary to make any comment on either. The red line represents the intended line of Railway on both Sections. I am sorry I could not attend the meeting but I hope Mr Steel will be able to make any explanation that may be wanted. I am very confident that the line I have laid out is the best that can be got.

I am Gentlemen

Your obt Sert

Geo: Stephenson

Professor Jack Simmons, who made the transcript, comments:

Nothing could show more clearly Stephenson's calm, and well-justified, self-confidence. He was the pioneer, who struggled with the technical problems of the railways, solved them to his own satisfaction, and expected his employers and associates to accept his solutions. They usually did.

The date of this letter is worth noting; it was written before the Stockton & Darlington was opened or the Liverpool & Manchester was authorized.

With all these gifts, it is comforting to remember that as an old man he had his own kind of eccentricity: he spent a good deal of time and ingenuity at his house at Tapton, near Chesterfield, on trying to persuade cucumbers to grow straight. In the end he forced them to, by encasing them in glass tubes. His son Robert, a very great and bold civil engineer, roundly declared, well knowing the ground and the problems involved, that the notion of a canal across the isthmus of Suez was commercially impracticable. But both of them triumphantly carried through what they set their hands to.

Stephenson's great contemporaries in civil engineering, Telford and Rennie, made little direct contribution to railways. It was the generation of engineers treading hard upon his heels – many of them his own pupils or associates, headed by his son Robert – that stamped the railways with the image they bore throughout the age of steam.

Robert Stephenson was in externals a somewhat gentler version of his father, but he lacked nothing in talent or administrative capacity, and his supreme ability was to work with people and inspire their confidence. He began his career in management of the engine factory set up by George at Newcastle, and from there he contributed much by way of refinement and detailed improvement to the rapidly-developing steam locomotive; then he was pushed forward by his father, who had a high and perfectly well-justified opinion of his son's abilities, to be chief engineer to a number of projects. The London & Birmingham was the most trying, and the Chester & Holyhead the grandest, of Robert Stephenson's lines. He travelled to South America, Egypt, and Canada; and in a strange encounter he met the less fortunate Trevithick, by then (1827) 'Don Ricardo', engineer to a rickety copper-mining concern, at Cartagena. He lived in London society, was M.P. for Whitby (a high Tory), and became F.R.S. It is difficult to penetrate to the man through the heavy varnish of the official biography; but Robert Stephenson seems to have been the most attractive of the handful of great railway engineers in the great age.

Isambard Kingdom Brunel was his great rival in life, and he rivals him in stature, even when seen from a century later. Brunel's talents were brilliant; at times they amounted almost to genius. He could exercise great personal charm and communicate his own enthusiasms to his associates. When Macaulay ran into the Athenaeum one day, crying 'It's out!', everyone knew what he meant: not another volume of the *History of England*, but the sovereign that had lodged in Brunel's windpipe. The engineer, speechless, had motioned for pencil and paper and forthwith designed an apparatus to swing him to and fro until the coin should be dislodged. The man was unbelievably fertile in ideas, always quick to question accepted practices and propose a better way of dealing with familiar problems. Too quick, perhaps: the Great Western directors took a fatal step when in 1835 they allowed their brilliant, persuasive young engineer to convince them that they should adopt the broad gauge of seven feet for their line. There were, and still are, most compelling technical arguments in favour of it; but one thing ought to have been decisive to the contrary – it was already too late. George Stephenson, with his usual heavy sagacity, had advised the Leicester & Swannington directors so six years before. The idea of the broad gauge was not impracticable – indeed, it was eminently practical; but in the long run the broad gauge could not keep a whole sector of the country to itself, and the flaw was fatal. Robert Stephenson, with his more earth-bound understanding, saw this clearly; Brunel would never admit it. The broad gauge was a failure not of technique but of administrative imagination. This was made clear in 1856, when a narrow-gauge rail had to be laid in the broad main line from Oxford to Reading and on to Basingstoke to give a through connexion from the north to the narrow-gauge South Western, by Act of Parliament; but it took another thirty-six years, until 1892, before the Great Western would face the end of the broad gauge.

Some of Brunel's other technical enthusiasms – the atmospheric railway and longitudinal timbers instead of cross-sleepers beneath the rails, for example – did not prove sound, and Robert Stephenson criticized them at the time. Yet their professional rivalry, which was intense, did not impair the close friendship between the two men; and the railway scene of the sixties was the poorer for their premature deaths, Robert Stephenson's in 1859 at the age of fifty-five, Brunel's in the same year at fifty-three.

The next year carried off another from the first rank of railway engineers – Joseph Locke, at the age of fifty-five. How these men had worn themselves out! Locke was one of George Stephenson's assistants on the Liverpool & Manchester and had then shown such ability that he won the appointment of engineer to the Grand Junction Railway, which was to be the link from the L. & M. southwards to Birmingham. It was a great undertaking, and the line was completed and opened throughout in June 1837. Without including any such sensational works as the Kilsby tunnel on the London & Birmingham or the great river-crossings that were soon to be tackled elsewhere, it was well laid and is recognizably a great line still; and – a real distinction – it was built within the engineer's original estimate of cost. Locke's other main lines were the London & Southampton, whose long swing over the Hampshire chalk between Basingstoke and Winchester bears the mark of classic railway building, and the Caledonian northwards from Carlisle, where he showed himself less terrified of a gradient than his contemporaries were. He was also responsible for several railways on the continent of Europe – between Paris and Le Havre and between Mantes and Cherbourg; from Barcelona to Mataró; and the Dutch Rhenish Railway.

With Locke, Thomas Brassey deserves also to be remembered. Brassey was not an engineer but the greatest of the race of railway engineering contractors. Before Brassey, railway contractors come to notice only because they so often went bankrupt; Brassey organized the business and made it a reputable branch of the profession. First on his own account, and then in association with Sir Morton Peto and E. L. Betts, Brassey undertook a vast number of railway contracts in the British Isles and overseas. His men were to be seen in almost every English county in the forties and fifties, and they struck genuine and unaffected terror into the hearts of the French during the construction of the line from Le Havre through Rouen to Paris.

One more who may perhaps without injustice be mentioned in this company is Vignoles. Charles Vignoles was an army officer discharged in the economies after Waterloo who turned to civil engineering and was engaged very early on the Liverpool & Manchester Railway – perhaps indeed as early as the spring of 1824, before even George Stephenson had produced his first scheme. He was engineer to the Midland Counties Railway (Leicester to Derby and Nottingham), opened in 1839; but he had a masterful and impetuous temperament and did not work happily with other engineers. His biggest work was the Sheffield, Ashton-under-Lyne & Manchester Railway (the nucleus of the later Great Central), with the Woodhead Tunnel, three miles long, as its principal feature; but he had to retire from it because of disagreement with the board after a financial imprudence on his part, which had nothing to do with his engineering ability. From this time onwards, though he did important work in Russia, he fell into the background, and he never rose to the same influence as Locke. Nevertheless, he possessed a vigorous talent.

Biographies of all these men have been written, but none of them (except the life of Brunel by Lady Noble) brings the railway engineer before our eyes as well as two portraits by Anthony Trollope. Sir Roger Scatcherd, in *Doctor Thorne*, and Theodore Burton, in *The Claverings*, are not major characters in the novelist's drama, and the professional side of their lives is touched on only by implication; yet Scatcherd is the very picture of a successful, overbearing railway contractor, and Burton of a Victorian civil engineer, with his strong character and conscientious approach to the business of life – 'full up to the eyes with good sense'. Perhaps that was the supreme quality of the best of them – good sense multiplied to such a power that it touched greatness.

Chapter 4

The task in Britain and the great years

The story of the physical extension of railways over the mainland of Britain has often been told, in outline and in detail; and it needs more than a few pages in an essay like this to do justice to it. Broadly, it falls into well-defined chapters: the beginnings and the first, heroic period of growth up to 1850; then the lean years of the fifties and a second great outburst of activity, which collapsed as much else did in 1866; third, a period of filling-in which lasted until 1910, when most of the remaining great water obstacles were overcome; and last, since then, new construction practically confined to urban and suburban lines. This section does not try to describe the process or even to chronicle its principal events. It tries rather to bring out certain significant tendencies by citing selected examples.

The first period, up to 1850, has just been called the 'heroic' period. What justification can there be for calling so commonplace a thing as railway building in Britain, involving no extremities of climate or fighting with hostile savages, 'heroic'? It lies in two things: the immense faith and will-power of the capitalists and constructors, and their organizing ability.

By the end of 1850, there were some 6,000 miles of railway open for public traffic in Great Britain. In 1830 there had been fewer than 100. In the five years from 1 January 1846 to 31 December 1850, over 3,600 miles of line had been opened, and at the beginning of 1851 a considerable further mileage was authorized and under construction. Much of this mileage carried double track; exactly how much is not recorded, but certainly more than half. London was by then connected with Birmingham, Manchester, and Liverpool by the London & North Western from Euston; and Scottish traffic was running on through Preston and Carlisle. At Rugby the Midland system branched off, leading on to Sheffield, Leeds, York, and Newcastle. During 1850 the Great Northern began running from London to Peterborough, and the 'East Coast' route of the future was taking shape. Dover, Brighton, Portsmouth, and Dorchester were all connected with London; the broad gauge extended through Bristol to Plymouth, and through Gloucester to Cheltenham. In East Anglia, passengers could ride from Shoreditch to Norwich, Yarmouth, and Lowestoft either via Colchester and Ipswich or by way of Cambridge and Ely; and from Ely they could reach the Midlands through Peterborough and Melton Mowbray. They could go by train to Lincoln and Grimsby, to Hull, Scarborough, and Whitby. There were three railway routes between Lancashire and the West Riding. There was rail connexion between north and west, by Birmingham and Bristol, interrupted by a regrettable 'break of gauge', involving change of carriage for all, at Gloucester. The South Wales Railway was open (though not connected with the Great Western until the Chepstow bridge was completed in 1852); the Chester & Holyhead carried the mails throughout to Holyhead for the steamer to Kingstown. Edinburgh could be reached via Newcastle and Berwick or by the Annandale route from Carlisle; the later 'Waverley Route' was at this time open only as far south as Hawick. From Glasgow the traveller to England had the choice of lines via Edinburgh, Carstairs, or Dumfries. Northwards in Scotland the rails stretched up the east coast to Aberdeen, but to reach Dundee the passenger from Edinburgh had to undergo ferry crossings of the Firths of Forth and Tay. North and west of Aberdeen there were plans but no railways.

Three of the companies overshadowed the rest: the London & North Western, a great amalgamation of railways whose line now stretched from Euston to Carlisle, a massive, well-established, ably-managed concern; the Great Western, with its broad gauge, higher speeds, and pushful policy, a sore trial on the left flank of the North Western and not yet assailed on its own left by the tiresome London & South Western; and the Midland, still a provincial railway with no independent access to London but commanding a wealthy district from its headquarters at Derby and well poised for breaking out in any direction. Another, the Great Northern, began effective competition during the year and would soon attack the North Western and the Midland from the east side and form the southern link in the 'East Coast' route.

There was through running between lines of the same gauge; passengers and goods were booked through, and the money was distributed through a clearing-house to which most of the important companies already belonged. Government kept a watchful eye on the operation of railways through the railway inspecting officers of the Board of Trade, and Parliament decided which lines ought to be sanctioned.

A national railway network was thus in being, and it was sufficiently well integrated and linked with the body politic to justify it being called a railway system. Not only was this system in being, it was also being used intensively. The total receipts in 1850 amounted to over £13 millions. Passenger traffic, which was viewed in prospect by the earliest promoters as secondary to goods and minerals, leaped in the early years to unimagined heights; in 1843 it represented almost seventy per cent of the total receipts, though in 1850 the freight total had come almost level with it. The next year, 1851, would witness an amazing movement of persons of all social classes to London for the Great Exhibition; this was the railway's social revolution. The countryman who had been to London was not likely to resemble a peasant, even in those districts where perhaps he did so in the earlier part of the century.

The physical achievement of all this construction was massive. The rolling and transport of rails alone was an immense task. The weight of iron in a mile of single track, in rails, chairs, and other fittings, at this time was about 156 tons. Making allowance for double track and sidings, each route mile of line must have required 300 or more tons of iron. Thus in the five years 1846 to 1850 (inclusive), when 4,000 miles of line were opened in the British Isles, and making some allowance for the locomotives (of which about 2,000 were at work by 1850, weighing some 25 tons each), for the iron components of rolling stock, bridges and structural work of various kinds, and for maintenance of tracks built earlier, it cannot be supposed that less than a million and a half tons of iron went into railways in those five years. This was more than the total output of iron in Great Britain in the year 1844. The annual British output was rising from 1.4 million tons in 1844 to 2 million tons in 1850, but exports (especially for railways overseas) were taking something like a quarter of this, so the home market for iron was dominated by the railway demands; and the iron-masters kept up with the demand. In the same five years, one may calculate that some 12 million timber sleepers were required for new lines alone; and as the average life of a sleeper was not above twelve years, there was a substantial quantity also wanted for replacements in the 2,600 miles already open by the end of 1844. Carriages and wagons, buildings, and sheds also required large amounts of timber for their construction. The sleepers and much of the other wood had to be imported from the Baltic lands. May this fact not have had some influence on opinions about relations with Russia in the early fifties?

It is clear that manufacturing achievement, and directing skill and organization, were deployed on an unprecedented scale. So also were the financial operations that made them possible; and here, in the eyes both of contemporaries and of later historians, lay the unsavoury part of the business. It is usual, and justifiable, to select the figure of George Hudson as characteristic of this period: the ill-bred, swaggering railway promoter whose dazzling career proved to rest upon insecure foundations, whose abounding confidence led him into disregard of ordinary financial rules and sometimes into downright dishonesty. A few years after he had disappeared from the public scene, he was taken to be a kind of swindler; by 1859 he was exhibited as the principal character of a rogues' gallery in a book by D. Morier Evans called *Facts, Failures, and Frauds*.

Hudson was by origin a York tradesman who came by the force of his own character and abilities to control the affairs of numerous different railway companies which roughly corresponded with the later Midland, Great Eastern, and North Eastern Railways. He carried through the first big amalgamation in English railway history – that of the North Midland, Midland Counties, and Birmingham & Derby Junction Railways – in 1844, and rose to the wealth and influence that could support a house in Albert Gate, facing Hyde Park (now the French Embassy), and the acquaintance of Prince Albert. But by 1849 committees of inquiry were reporting to the shareholders of Hudson's companies that much was amiss in their financial affairs; so the great man, spurned by all who had flattered him, withdrew with dignity to an obscure exile. His failings were exposed for all to see, though even in 1851 John Francis could write, while condemning him:

Let him be thought of as one who, more sinned against than sinning, has been a scapegoat for the sins of the many; and let it, too, be considered that he has done the state some service, and may yet do it much more.

In that prophecy Mr Francis was wrong; but when Hudson died in 1871, *The Times* wrote that he was 'a man who united largeness of view with wonderful speculative courage – the kind of man who leads the world.'

What was the nature of Hudson's service to the British railway system, which could still be remembered amid the outcry from the virtuous who pursued him? It was that, among the cheerily optimistic, or absolutely fraudulent, railway promoters of the boom years in the middle forties, he, the most powerful of them all, insisted on promoting only those lines that were genuinely meant to be built. This was an important and distinctive attitude. Second, he attempted to secure useful amalgamations – a policy that Parliament and public opinion generally was reluctant to accept until after the 1914–18 war, but one that if adopted much earlier might well have led to good results. Third, he did try to secure economical working and management of the lines he controlled – not always, it must be said, with success. Nevertheless, it is probably true to say that without Hudson's insistence on these three principles, and his powerful leadership in support of them, the aftermath of 1845 in the railway world would have been chaotic indeed.

As it was, the railways in 1850, when the pace was slackening, could point to a tolerably sensible system of lines. They were accepted by the public as a normal feature of social life. Parliament had accommodated its antique procedure to the enormous mass of business thrust upon it by the railways, and the machine had not broken down. Finance and manufactures had adapted themselves to the extraordinary demands made upon them; there was a sense of exhilaration, and perhaps some strain, in the economy, but a workable railway system was there, and Hudson had done much to create it. Only Belgium, among countries in similar conditions, could show any parallel to this development. In France, by contrast, government and capitalists dithered and delayed, even when the revolution of 1848 was not filling their minds. In the end, no doubt, France got a well-devised, planned railway system, but its development was so slow that the country's economy slipped back significantly in comparison with Britain's, where, in spite of mistakes and misjudgements, the furious energy of the railway builders had by the middle of the nineteenth century driven Britain ahead for the moment out of reach of her manufacturing and commercial rivals.

But had the price been too high? It is common, among railwaymen and the public alike, to believe that it was so. The growth of the railway system in Britain is often referred to as though the whole business was a rather shady speculation, in which a few individuals made large fortunes and then deservedly crashed. It has been said so often that it has become almost a truism that the railways were laid out in an ill-conceived fashion which owed nothing to intelligent foresight and that consequently they have groaned ever since under an unjustifiable burden of capital charges. The Labour Party, for example, in an official policy pamphlet of 1955, could write:

> Even after Parliamentary sanction had been obtained, the railways still had to pay exorbitant prices for the land on which to lay their track, and submit themselves to costly restrictions at the whim of the landowners. … Interest on this grossly inflated expenditure was a continual burden on railway receipts.

There is nothing peculiar to the Labour Party in this view of railway history – it is a recent expression of what many well-informed people have believed to be the facts of the matter. Lord Stamp, when he was president of the L.M.S. Railway, allowed himself to use the expression 'the blackmails of the forties', though he went on to say that it was easy to exaggerate this element in British railway costs. It is easy, and it is often done. It is probably too late to do much about altering the belief, even though it is wrong; but the tale deserves to be looked at more closely.

Difficult negotiations and hard bargains there certainly were, and there were celebrated examples of what looked very much like extortion from the companies. Lord Petre, of Ingatestone Hall in Essex, is said to have received £120,000 for land worth at most £5,000 on the Eastern Counties line. This is an often-cited case, and research into the family papers may provide some reason to modify the story; but the point is that it was, and still is, believed. In another way, too, the railways are thought to have suffered – at the hands of the lawyers: Charles Austin made something like £50,000 in the single year 1847 from railway business alone. Does the sum of all these things represent an intolerable and continuing burden, or when spread over all the immense investment did it come down to some insignificant proportion?

The only modern writer who has gone into this question thoroughly, Mr Harold Pollins, has assembled a reasonably full amount of statistical evidence on these points. This has shown that between 1825 and 1850 the twenty-seven principal railway companies spent some £50 million on construction (in its widest sense); of this, the total expenditure on land was almost £7 million – about 13.9 per cent – and the preliminary expenses, including the general costs of promotion and Parliamentary costs, were in nearly all cases less than 5 per cent of the whole. These are not intolerable proportions; even if they had been rather higher, one might still think them reasonable. This does not mean that no landlords were paid excessively; but it does show that the somewhat eager or excessive payments so often quoted were singular and not characteristic.

It is a pity that detailed investigations of this kind by an economic historian are not likely to be noticed by controversialists. It is probably far too late now for the myth ever to be overtaken by the facts of the matter; but it is valuable to have it on record that, in relation to the total investment of £1,100 millions in British railways, those picturesque episodes in the eighteen-forties have no significance. The result, so solid and well founded, so swiftly produced, remains for us to admire. The plain facts are impressive enough. With a little imagination, the feat of production and organization that lay behind them can be recognized as prodigious; with a little more imagination, and some charity towards an unpopular set of men, the practical faith of the capitalists can be approved, and even envied.

Viewed against the background of early Victorian England, in which so much remained from earlier ages that was hostile to this development or did nothing to assist it, the achievement must look remarkable. Viewed from the late twentieth century, when we struggle confusedly to decide on any consensus for transport, the Victorian who created the railways look like a race imbued with some daemonic energy.

Chapter 5

Completing the task

After 1850, a chill wind was felt whistling about the railway boardrooms, and the pace of construction slowed down. Money was diffficult to find to pay for the expensive promises of the late forties, and everything sobered up. The fifties were far less rumbustious in the railway world; and yet there were some signs of what was just ahead. Competing lines like those from London to Portsmouth and to Chatham and Dover (which gave rise to the most desperate sustained railway rivalry of the century) were developed or developing by 1860; the Midland got an entry into London, for which Bedfordshire owners sold land at no more than its agricultural value. Amalgamations went forward, producing in 1854 the giant North Eastern, in 1862 the Great Eastern, in 1863 a much greater Great Western; and all was ready for another railway boom in 1864–6. This time there were differences from the 1845 'mania'. There was a boom, certainly, and money was seeking an outlet; but very much of the railway activity of the middle sixties was worked up by contractors, who engaged themselves in the financing of new lines. Sir Morton Peto and Thomas Brassey appeared among them – disastrously for Peto, who went bankrupt when the affairs of the London, Chatham & Dover went crashing down after the collapse of the Overend, Gurney bank and the ensuing commercial crisis of 1866. The great established railway companies became involved in this uprush of activity, many of them against their will and simply in order to defend their own territories against violent invasion; but some, like the London, Brighton & South Coast, engaged in particularly ill-judged speculations. A product of this period, though not put into operation until 1875, was the third route to Scotland, the Midland's grand and costly moorland line from Settle to Carlisle. It was promoted by the Midland, which had as its allies for the occasion the Lancashire & Yorkshire and the North British.

On the morning after, the Midland wanted to get out of its commitment; but the allies, who had nothing to lose, held the Midland to its task. Elsewhere, the Midland needed no second bidding to jump into fresh competition – in South Wales, Manchester, and the eastern counties; and this period, succeeding the age of the pioneers, may well be called the age of the interlopers.

It was also the age when railways were carried to the fringes of Britain – the margins which had been left outside the pattern of 1850. The ends of Cornwall were reached in 1859; railways in the Isle of Wight date from this period. Central Wales was criss-crossed with single lines of railway, eking out a tenuous living, by 1870, though the silliest proposal of all those seriously made, to build over the mountains from Shrewsbury to a small bay called Porth Dinllaen on the Caernarvonshire coast, was not pursued. (A sort of *ignis fatuus* darted about over this place, considered by some to offer great possibilities for rivalling Holyhead in the Irish trade.) In Scotland, Aberdeen and Perth were linked with Inverness, and the metals were carried through the Highlands to Strome Ferry, reached in 1870, and well on the way to Wick and Thurso. Southward from Edinburgh, the 'Waverley Route' through Galashiels and Hawick was opened through to Carlisle in 1862; but the East Coast traveller going northwards had still to face the rigours of two ferry-passages to get to Dundee.

By 1870, the railway map of Britain, with 13,500 miles on it, showed not only in outline but also in its details most of the twentieth-century system. North Norfolk was hardly touched, or North Devon and Cornwall – and there was more to come in Wales and Scotland; but the traveller to most places was not ill-served, so far as actual provision of railways went, in 1870. After that date – in many ways the turning-point of the Victorian age – there were certainly important additions: interlopers like the Hull & Barnsley, the Barry in South Wales, the Midland's assault on Manchester, the South-Western's advance to Plymouth and Padstow, the Cheshire Lines' route between Liverpool and Manchester; lines on the very margin of conceivable profitability, like the West Highland, northwards from the Firth of Clyde across the bleak Moor of Rannoch to Fort William; new cut-offs, like the Great Western's bold and successful construction which removed the reproach that its initials 'G.W.R.' stood for 'Great Way Round'; and the last main line to London, the Great Central. In Scotland, the great east-coast firths were bridged; the Severn was tunnelled. But, except for the cut-offs, railways built since 1870 outside suburban or new industrial areas are mostly suspect as economic propositions; probably they always should have been. The last to be thought of, they are proving the first to go. Cross-country lines like the Midland & Great Northern in Lincolnshire and Norfolk, or the Midland & South Western Junction running north and south across Wiltshire, paid nothing or very little in the heyday of the rail. The Golden Valley Railway in south-west Herefordshire – 'unfortunate, puffed up by over-optimism, but humbly useful' – cost about £335,000 to build in the 1870s and 1880s; the Great Western got it for £9,000 in 1898. It was not uniquely unfortunate. The country branch line built since 1870 has to be unusually situated to be able to justify itself when motor-cars and lorries are ranged against it.

As early as the sixties, an Act of Parliament in 1864 had laid down an economical procedure by which railways of primarily local interest could be promoted, and another of 1868 provided for different operating standards in respect of 'light' railways; but the powers were not then used extensively. Between 1896 and 1914, however, there was a certain amount of hopeful activity in sub-standard railways, either on narrow gauges or built to lighter standards of construction. The hopes were generally disappointed; to be any use, a branch line needed to be part of the parent system, so that rolling stock could be worked through without special restrictions. The railway is not an efficient transport agency for sparse traffic, and the areas still away from the main network could not be expected to yield traffic that was much better than sparse. There was, of course, a good deal of discussion about how far the contribution made by the branches to the traffic on the main lines should be taken into account in estimating their value; but this factor, if it could be evaluated, would probably never have offset the clear losses of the branch lines which were in those generally affluent times not separately calculated. But the interesting question has never been settled, and the discussion continues.

In the latest period, the mere addition of route-mileage to the map has ceased to be a valuable index of railway activity: intensity of use was not now connected with length of line. It was the development of traffic facilities on the existing lines that mattered – extra tracks, better signalling, flying junctions to avoid conflicting train movements, better terminals, and in the right places – London, Merseyside, Manchester, Tyneside – electrification. In the greatest cities – London, Liverpool, Glasgow – underground railways, steam-operated in the earlier versions, were called for and justified by the exceptional passenger traffic problems; elsewhere, some new suburban lines and a good many new stations were built. Not everyone saw that the railway-building age was over: even the evident failure of the Great Central's extension to London (in a commercial sense) could not deter people from proposing rival lines from Bristol to London (in 1902) and from London to Brighton (also in 1902) and between Manchester and Liverpool (a monorail scheme of 1900). But there was already quite enough railway in Britain – the total was 20,281 route miles by 1913; and the time had come to start weeding out the parts that were not wanted by any reasonable test. That process, after a premature start during the 1914–18 war, would really begin after 1922–3, when four 'grouped' companies took over and operated the properties of over 120 former separate concerns; and it continued more rapidly since 1948, when unification into one 'British Railways' and a harsher climate of economy made the process at once easier to carry through on a common basis and more necessary if the railways were to come near making both ends meet, or even to show that there was no demonstrable waste of the community's resources in the provision of services considered to be socially desirable.

Chapter 6

The impact of railways on society

The physical achievement of building the British railway system was remarkable, and especially so in the earlier years. In the early years also it could be seen that the result of building them was nothing less than a social revolution. Sydney Smith put it in his own fashion, in 1842:

> Railroad travelling is a delightful improvement of human life. Man is become a bird; he can fly quicker and longer than a Solan goose The mamma rushes sixty miles in two hours to the aching finger of her conjugating and declining grammar boy. The early Scotchman scratches himself in the morning mists of the north, and has his porridge in Piccadilly before the setting sun … Everything is near, everything is immediate – time, distance, and delay are abolished.

But he went on to talk about accidents, and suggested that if a bishop were burnt to death in a railway smash much improvement would result.

In its less ebullient fashion, *The Times* examined railway statistics in 1850:

> There are thousands of our readers, we are sure, who, in the last three years of their lives, have travelled more and seen more than in all their previous life taken together. Thirty years ago not one countryman in one hundred had seen the metropolis. [How did *The Times* know this?] There is now scarcely one in the same number who has not spent the day there. Londoners go in swarms to Paris for half the sum, and in one-third of the time, which in the last reign it would have cost them to go to Liverpool. The manufacturers of Yorkshire and Lancashire are carried by shoals to the lakes of Cumberland. The agriculturists of the eastern counties are deposited in droves at Yarmouth.

Next year, in 1851, the Great Exhibition presented its challenge to the railways and gave them their chance to show dramatically that they were equal – more than equal – to the unprecedented demands made on their passenger facilities. As the exhibition buildings were being dismantled in October, *The Times* reflected in a leader on the figures of attendance. There had been 6,200,000 separate visits; of these, only about 75,000 were made by foreigners. A very fair proportion of the people came from the Midlands and the North.

> Now, how did they come? Had it been proposed thirty years ago, or even twenty-five years ago, to get up an exhibition in London, on the speculation that three million persons would come to it, and half a million of money would be taken at the doors, the most practical men of the day would have laughed the proposition to scorn. When it was rumoured during the Reform Bill that fifty thousand men from Birmingham were about to present a petition in person, a great authority asked, 'Where will they find shoes?'

(It is not difficult to guess who 'the great authority' must have been; it sounds very much like the Duke of Wellington.)

Railway traffic of all kinds had grown with fantastic speed. The growth in passenger traffic, and its diversion from the turnpike roads to new, unfamiliar routes, caused local difficulties of an embarrassing kind; thus, as early as 1838, the following dire news was reported from Birmingham:

> So much has the opening of the London & Birmingham Railway increased the number of travellers through this town that the principal inns often have their beds engaged two days deep; and last week so great was the difficulty of procuring accommodation that the Countess of Chesterfield was obliged to sleep at the Acorn, in Temple Street.

On the goods side, the change took a little longer, and the canals were not snuffed out with the dramatic suddenness of the stage-coaches' disappearance; some, indeed, were not snuffed out at all. But, though established trades took some few years to transfer their traffic to rail, new ones were quick to seize their chances. By 1848 the Eastern Counties Railway was bringing seventy tons of fresh fish a week into London from Yarmouth and Lowestoft, laying the foundation of a new trade and a new kind of diet for those who lived away from the seaboard.

With travel went news. The Paris Bourse was astonished to receive at 1.30 p.m., on 11 December 1849, *The Times* of the same morning, which had been dispatched from London at 7 a.m. This was a special effort, put on to make publicity for the South Eastern and Nord railways' routes; but the London newspapers were then regularly catching the 6 a.m. 'newspaper expresses' from Euston and Paddington. In 1875, the time went back to 5.15 a.m., which brought London papers to Manchester by 10. In 1899, the new Great Central put on a train from Marylebone for the *Daily Mail* at 2.30 a.m.

On the other hand, the collection of news meant telegraphs. The first public use of the electric telegraph was on the Great Western Railway, between West Drayton and Paddington. The railway and the electric telegraph went together; in 1854, out of seventeen metropolitan offices of the Electric Telegraph Company eight were at railway termini, and in the country the telegraph office was almost invariably at the railway station. Still, on important occasions the telegraph had to be supplemented, and in 1862 an engine was kept with steam up at Holyhead waiting to carry up the reply of the United States Government to the British dispatch on the *Trent* case. It waited from 2 to 9 January, and then the dispatch arrived. With one stop at Stafford, the tiny little engines of that day, which were sometimes brought to a stand by high winds on the North Wales coast, arrived at Euston in five hours: 264 miles at an average speed of 52¾ miles an hour, a prodigious speed for the time over so great a distance.

The Post Office was not slow to make use of railways for conveyance of mails. It began on the Liverpool & Manchester line in November 1830 – a marked sign of confidence in the new method of transport – and letter-sorting carriages appeared on trains in 1838. Pick-up apparatus for receiving and dispatching mailbags at intermediate points with the train in motion was invented and first used in the same year. The young Piedmontese Camillo Cavour, visiting England in 1843 and travelling a lot on the railways, noted that several carriages were needed for letters, whereas one had sufficed a few years before. The relations of the railways and the Post Office were always close, and frequently inharmonious; the Postmaster General was always pushing the railways rather faster than they wanted to go.

In particular, the conveyance of mails brought one very bothersome matter to a head: Sunday travel. In the Victorian era it would have been considered scandalously inefficient to have no delivery of letters in towns on a Sunday, and the Post Office was adamant that mail trains must be run on Sunday as well as on weekdays. A fierce debate arose about the propriety of Sunday travelling, whose echoes were heard at shareholders' meetings, in Parliament, and all over Scotland and Wales throughout the nineteenth century. The fact that mail trains had to be run on the main lines really settled the issue in favour of the Sunday travellers from the start, but the opposition was dogged. Some shareholders declined to accept the proportion of their dividends which they calculated had been earned on Sundays, and on the London & North Western the funds thus made available were devoted to schools set up by the company for the children of the employees in the workshops at Crewe and Wolverton and at other places. In the 1830s the Liverpool & Manchester paid money from its Sunday travel fund to charities.

The fierce indignation felt by some sections of the community against Sunday travelling did not quickly expire. The villagers of Loch-Carron-side, armed with sticks and clubs, took complete possession of Strome Ferry pier and station, on the Highland Railway, on Sunday, 3 June 1883, and managed to foil an attempt to land fish and dispatch it by train to the south. When ten of the men involved returned home from Calton Jail, Edinburgh, after their prison sentences had been remitted, they were received like heroes. Opposition was not confined to Scotland: as late as 1889 the Anti-Sunday Travel Union had fifty-eight branches, in different parts of the country, and some 8,000 adherents. Partly owing to its activities, trains on suburban lines normally ceased running on Sundays during the hours of divine service – a practice of which traces could be seen in some London timetables down to the 1914 war, and even later. The Caledonian Railway got into trouble for running a Sunday steamer to Clyde coast resorts in 1909; and in the same year the Rev. Lord Blythswood testified that he had never used a public conveyance on the Lord's Day for nearly fifty years, although this had prevented him from preaching in many places.

The railway timetable first made Greenwich time standard throughout the country. Early time-sheets have footnotes converting local time to Greenwich; it must have been a tiresome business. For example, on the Great Western timetable of 30 July 1841 it is noted: 'London time is about 4 min. earlier than Reading time, 7½ min. before Cirencester, and 14 min. before Bridgwater.' The directors had minuted in 1840 that London time was to be used throughout the G.W. system; but it was not until 1852 that the telegraph was completed along the main lines so that time signals could be transmitted regularly from London. Nevertheless, traditions continued even after the installation of telegraphs; a specially-regulated watch was sent down daily from Euston to Holyhead by which the departure of the mail steamer was timed. This went on until 1939. 'Railway time' (or London time) rapidly spread from the stations into the villages and towns, which naturally conformed, and it quickly became all but universal. Only a few clocks, like the one on Christ Church cathedral at Oxford, still show the local time.

Uniformity of time was a symptom of a much closer conformity of manners and social life throughout the country, as travelling, and especially touring, brought the remoter and more backward districts into constant touch with the other parts. The 'Wild Wales' that George Borrow had known disappeared during the sixties, when the Cambrian and Central Wales lines were pushed through the heart of Merioneth, Montgomery, and Radnor; and when writers like Wilkie Collins set out for 'Rambles Beyond Railways' they found it hard to escape from their influence anywhere on the British mainland. Greater conformity there was; but the railways did not ever look like imposing anything resembling uniformity of speech and manners throughout the whole country. It has been left to broadcasting and television to do that. In one outward respect, however, railways did swamp regional traditions – in building, by carrying Fletton bricks all over the country and distributing Welsh slates from the seaports, so that one sort of house became the cheapest to build anywhere between Carlisle and Dover. There are plenty of examples clustered round most railway stations.

The railway, then, induced a general approximation of the habits and thoughts of all parts of the kingdom; was it also in its effects egalitarian? There were those who viewed its earliest efforts and were certain that it would be so. Thus, one Mr Prentice, a Manchester man, wrote:

The opening of the Manchester and Liverpool Railway was one of the events of 1830 which was not without its influence in future days on the progress of public opinion. The anti-corn-law agitation was wonderfully forwarded by quick railway travelling and the penny postage. Even in 1830 the railway promoted the cause of reform. It was an innovation on the old ways of travelling, and a successful one; and people thought that something like this achievement in constructive and mechanical science might be effected in political science. It brought, besides, a little proprietary borough, which nobody had ever seen before, into full view. I recollect when passing over it for the first time, I said to a friend: 'Parliamentary reform must follow soon after the opening of this road. A million of persons will pass over it in the course of this year and see that hitherto unseen village of Newton; and they must be convinced of the absurdity of its sending two members to Parliament whilst Manchester sends none.'

Mr Prentice, and plenty of other people who thought like him, were really expecting too much of the railway. It is true that in 1832 Manchester got its seats and Newton was disfranchised; but the movement that led to the Reform Act was in full force before the railway began to exhibit the trifling extent of Newton-le-Willows to the passing thousands. It has not been by direct confrontation of political anomalies but by their indirect effects that improved means of travel and communication have exercised influence on political life. Movements of thought had spread very rapidly before the nineteenth century: Luther's Reformation swept over Germany in a shorter time than Hitler's revolution.

Directly, the railways did not have an egalitarian effect; if anything, it was rather the reverse. Almost immediately, they enabled the wealthier and middle classes to live at some distance from the places of their daily work; this helped to create sharp differences of class between the different parts of a city and its suburbs, which had not existed in the earlier age when 'good' town houses mostly lay close beside houses which were not good. The railway made it possible for Manchester merchants (the successful ones) to live at Alderley Edge, and Bradford men to live at Harrogate or Morecambe.

On the trains, and at stations, class distinctions were established and respected. First, second, and third were sharply distinguished, and a sort of fourth class appeared from time to time. (The case of the Keyham Dockyard Railway, with its five different classes, may be considered exceptional, as being a private concern of the Board of Admiralty and not a public railway.) Separate waiting rooms for each class, and separate dining rooms, were provided at all important stations. At Coupar Angus, on the Caledonian main line, there were still to be seen on the down platform first- and second-class waiting rooms, separately for ladies and gentlemen, in 1938, forty-five years after second class disappeared from the Scottish railways. The story of passenger classes is a curious one. Beginning with two classes (corresponding to 'inside' and 'outside' on the stage coaches), the railways soon found that a third was required and was commercially successful; then during the early period many varieties of accommodation and charging were tried. Although 'class' as applied to passenger travel is normally taken to denote the kind of accommodation provided in the carriage, other things can be involved also; principally admission to specific trains. By the time that main-line traffic began on any considerable scale at the end of the thirties, there were at least three classes of accommodation, and variations of fare within each class according to the speed of the trains.

Until the seventies the class and charging arrangements of the different railways remained diverse; some of them still charged 'express' fares by the best trains, which were in fact a supplement on the ordinary first and second. But a dramatic change was to take place. The Midland Railway had reached London over its own metals in 1868 and was determined to compete with the London & North Western and the Great Northern for passenger traffic; and it procceded to carry third-class passengers on some of its second-best fast trains. James Allport, the general manager, was convinced that the future lay with third class and one other; years before, in 1850, he had run first-and-third-only trains on the Manchester, Sheffield & Lincolnshire. As the essential first stop, third-class passengers were carried on all Midland trains from April 1872. Then in January 1875 the Midland abolished second class; or rather, without saying so, it abolished first class, for the new first-class fares were the same as the previous seconds. The other companies grumbled very loud, not so much at the disappearance of second as the reduction of first-class charges; but they followed suit in time – a big block including the Great Northern, North Eastern, and all the Scottish companies in 1893; the Great Western by 1910; the London & North Western in 1912 (so long as Lord Stalbridge was chairman, the proposal might not be raised). The southern lines were last (1912–23), except for some L.N.E.R. suburban lines. Continental boat trains maintained three classes until the same process took place on the continent; first class had been dwindling away for years, and it was declared dead in June 1956. Thereupon the old second and third became first and second; and British Railways moved third up to second, so as to be in line.

The superior class itself has not come through unscathed. The later tube railways never provided it, and 'rail-motorcars' for branch-line services introduced in the 1900s often dispensed with it. (Not so on the Great Central, where a single saloon vehicle for branch working contained four saloons: first and third class, smoking and no smoking.) During the Second World War all suburban services within thirty miles of London were reduced to third class only; but there does not yet appear any disposition to go further in this direction. Indeed, the beautiful simplicity of a single class is nowhere near achievement, for supplementary fares, either for high-speed trains or for superior accommodation or service on Pullman cars, have brought back multiplicity of different classes in a disguised form.

The three classes of early days were widely felt not to be enough, at both ends of the scale. A fourth class, not always so named, appeared on the Manchester & Leeds Railway in 1841, the Edinburgh & Glasgow in 1845, the Great Northern in 1848 (this to meet steamboat competition on the Witham Navigation), and later on the Norfolk Railway and the Great Western. On the other hand, aristocratic persons used to travel in their own carriages, lasted on flat wagons. The compartment railway carriage won acceptance among the upper classes only very slowly.

> At last [wrote Augustus Hare of his family journeys by rail about 1850] we came to use the ordinary railway carriage, but then for a long time we used to have post-horses to meet us at some station near London: my mother would not be known to enter London in a railway carriage – 'it was so excessively improper' (the sitting opposite strangers in the same carriage); so we entered the metropolis by land, as it was called in the early days of railway travelling.

During the seventies, Pullman or other saloon cars were introduced, and trains were put on formed of these cars, with supplementary fares to exclude the wrong sort of people. The Brighton line had some of these, including the 'City Limited' (not a Pullman train); this was the 5 p.m. first-class train from London Bridge, which, according to the London,

Brighton & South Coast Railway's Official Guide of 1912, 'conveys over three hundred merchant princes and others to their marine villas at Brighton'. The merchant princes of Manchester did not, however, remain content with plain first class, and they got the Lancashire & Yorkshire and London & North-Western Railways in the spacious Edwardian decade (and later) to run special saloon coaches, to which none but members of a club were admitted, between Manchester and Blackpool, Windermere, and Llandudno.

Nevertheless, the very routes on which these exclusive and expensive trains have run are those on which the mass of the populace has been carried at the lowest rates by the most characteristic product of the railway age: the excursion train. The excursion is something different from a further class of passenger accommodation: it is a service of a particular kind, in connexion with a particular occasion, at charges fixed for the occasion. Latterly, the word has been more and more widely stretched until 'excursion fare' denotes simply a lower rate of charge for travel by ordinary trains; but the excursion really signifies travel especially arranged for a particular event. On one interpretation, the first excursion took place on the Liverpool & Manchester line on the day after its formal opening. About 130 persons, most of them members of the Society of Friends on their way to their quarterly meeting at Manchester, travelled by a specially-provided train at the fare which became normal for public traffic from the following day. Something like an excursion took place on the remote Bodmin & Wadebridge line on 14 June 1836, when 800 passengers were handled. The idea became very popular in the North and the Midlands. The early excursions must have been astonishing affairs; it seems to have been usual for them to be welcomed at their destination by bands of music, and they were often enormously long, almost surpassing belief. The following report from Leicester is dated 24 August 1840:

> About half-past twelve o'clock this day a train, perhaps the longest ever known, came along the Midland Counties Railway from Nottingham. It had four engines to drag it forward, and to the beholder appeared like a moving street, the houses of which were filled with human beings … The number of carriages was 67, and the number of passengers nearly 3,000, most of whom were well and respectably attired.

Next year, on 5 July 1841, a very important event took place on this same railway; Mr Thomas Cook arranged an excursion from Leicester to Loughborough and back for a shilling a head, in connexion with a temperance demonstration. This was the foundation of that immense business of travel associated with his name; and it may be remarked that Mr Bell, secretary of the Midland Counties Railway Company, helped Thomas Cook to find the money to cover the preliminary expenses of that first trip. Thus early did the railway recognize the value of the travel agent. Cook on that day did not run the first railway excursion, but he did run the first excursion to be publicly advertised and sponsored by an agent.

It is curious how the temperance motif keeps cropping up throughout railway history. A pleasing example is the teetotallers' excursion from Redruth and Camborne to Hayle, by the West Cornwall Railway, in 1852; the train consisted of three engines and seventy-five broad-gauge carriages, and a song was written for the occasion, with the rousing chorus:

> Happy Camborne, happy Camborne,
>   Where the railway is so near,
> And the engine shows how water
>   Can accomplish more than beer.

Bands of music had appeared on railway stations before the first excursion trains: at the opening ceremonies. The collected accounts of these occasions would make a curious volume, both for the variety and usually the enormous length of the proceedings; and also because very few of them seem to have been got through as planned. The Liverpool & Manchester opening, as already mentioned, was badly mismanaged, apart from the death of Huskisson (which cannot be held against the railway); when the Duke of Wellington's special train arrived at Manchester, an ugly riot was prevented only by withdrawing him as swiftly as possible back along the railway. As the locomotives were in something of a muddle, and most of them were suffering from lack of water because of earlier delays, the only thing that could be done with the train was to attach it to an engine on the adjoining line by a chain and to pull it as far as Eccles, where another engine had watered and was waiting. All cross-over lines between the two tracks had been taken out for greater safety on that day.

Elsewhere, one reads of interminable dinners and speeches; they lasted five and a half hours at York, after a hard day inspecting the York & North Midland line, and a ball at the Guildhall followed. Many years later, in 1875, the opening of the line to New Radnor was celebrated by the public roasting of a Fat Ox; and when the South Devon Railway was extended from Torre to Torquay and Paignton in 1859 a riot developed about the sharing out of an immense pudding weighing 1½ tons which had been prepared for the occasion.

From the Royal Family downwards, people flocked to the railway: Prince Albert first used it in 1839, the Queen in 1842 from Slough to Paddington. She wrote to her Uncle Leopold that she was quite charmed with it. All ranks adopted it at once, even if with reservations like Mrs Hare's about the impropriety of certain features; the letters and diaries of the period do not record many die-hards who continued to travel by road to their country estates, even though some few might prefer to join the railway outside the Metropolis. How could they? The advantages in saving of time and energy were overwhelming. Cecil Torr, in his engaging book *Small Talk at Wreyland* (near Lustleigh, in South Devon), records the successive times from London to Wreyland in the forties: in 1841 his father 'started from Piccadilly in the *Defiance* coach at half-past four, stopped at Andover for supper and Ilminster for breakfast, and reached Exeter at half-past ten. Allowing for stops, this meant travelling about ten miles an hour.' The whole journey took 21 hours. In October 1842 he went as far as Taunton by train, and took 12¼ hours. In March 1845, by train to Exeter, he took 10¼ hours; in August 1846, catching the 9.45 a.m. express to Exeter, he took about 6½ hours. In 1846 he used the rail as far as Teignmouth, in 1847 to Newton Abbot. The coach fare to Exeter was £3 to £3. 10s., to which about a quarter had to be added in tips; the railway fare was then £2. 4s. 6d. first class, £2. 10s. express, and no tips. Few people could hold out against this combination of advantages; even one hunting neighbour of the Torrs, having to go to London on urgent business in 1851, committed his soul to its Creator, and took a ticket by the train.

The impact of the railway was overwhelming; it met the needs of the age, and did so much more than meet its needs that it created fresh opportunities and fresh demands of many kinds. Some public figures tried to stand up against its new popularity. The lone voice of Colonel

Sibthorp, M.P. for Lincoln ('an able but eccentric speaker', according to the *Concise D.N.B.*), can be faintly heard across the years: 'All railways are public frauds and private robberies.' He said, when Gladstone brought in his Regulation of Railways Bill in 1844, that he wished he was introducing a measure to annihilate them altogether.

But Sibthorp was almost alone. John Henry Newman listed, as one of the Liberal propositions which he earnestly denounced and abjured, the view that railroad travelling with education, periodical literature, ventilation, and the arts of life were things serving to make a population moral and happy. But the Liberals of 1840 had the vast majority of thinking men with them; steam power and the railway locomotive symbolized the secular aspirations of the age. In the early 1840s the west Cumberland town of Maryport acquired a third newspaper in addition to the *Maryport Advertiser* and the *Maryport Pacquet* (for provincial journalism proliferated, if it did not always flourish, in those days), and it was quite natural for the newcomer to be named the *Maryport Locomotive*. Again, *The Times* in 1840, commenting on an incident in the peculiar military career of Lord Cardigan, observed: 'Any unfortunate commoner with half such a rebuke would have been struck out of the army at railroad speed.' 'Railway' became a sort of cant word for 'modern', just as in our own age the word 'atomic' is used to impute to all sorts of objects (including fly-papers) the quality of being up to date, the very latest thing. Children's games and alphabets were based upon the railway; even music was brought in – 'The Excursion Train Galop', with a fine lithograph of the South Eastern Railway on the cover, was a favourite piece in the late forties. Railways struck the public imagination at once.

The railway was accepted as part of the social scene with astonishingly little difficulty. Up and down the country, people were prepared to welcome it. With a very few exceptions, towns wanted the railway; and many of the alleged exceptions can probably be shown to be apocryphal; Northampton and Uxbridge certainly can be. Kingston-on-Thames is not proven, but likely. Abingdon indeed kept out the Great Western's Oxford branch, and bitterly repented it; other towns, like Modbury and South Molton, in Devonshire, or Eccleshall, in Staffordshire, that were not lucky enough to be on a railway line just decayed. Most of the towns with any spirit – Moretonhampstead and Ashburton, for example, to take Devon again – promoted branches to the nearest main line, and got railway communication of a sort, which was much better than none. With a railway station, a place was linked with the national system; its name appeared in *Bradshaw* and the *A.B.C.*; it was on a limb of the main body. Without a railway, in the nineteenth century and indeed into our own times, a town or village is somehow cut off from the main stream of things. This is still obscurely felt in many places, which explains the frantic efforts to keep country branch-lines open which are so often made at the present time by people who never use them. The railway is regarded as a mark of civilization essential to the life of an area, and no amount of transport by road quite makes up for the lack of it. 'Take that mark of civilization and progress away, and we are a depressed area,' a Sedbergh taxi-driver is quoted as saying to the *Manchester Guardian* about the closing of the Lune Valley branch in 1953. (Taxi-drivers, and others, seem to become philosophical beyond their wont when talking to representatives of the *Guardian*.) The railway was a thing that people valued having, in its early days; and one that they still value, so long, very often, as other people will pay for it.

Chapter 7

Railways and the landscape

It may seem a curious thing, at first sight, that the railway slipped so easily into the landscape of Britain. In the earliest days, awe was excited by the stupendous scale of the great engineering works; but then it could be seen that the sweeping horizontal line of embankment and viaduct consorted quite well with the existing pattern of tidy field and hedgerow. The wayside station, with its neat station house, two sidings, four railwaymen's cottages, and attendant inn, fitted snugly into its surroundings; the level crossing, with its keeper's single-storeyed dwelling, that was visible for miles across the Fens was certainly no worse in its looks than the contemporary farms and cottages. So it happened that, in the early age, it was only in the mountains that much opposition was raised in defence of what would now be called the natural amenities. The *locus classicus* is Wordsworth on the Kendal & Windermere Railway:

> Is there no nook of English ground secure
> From rash assault?

he thundered. (Later he was pleased to discover that railway labourers could be gentle and pious men.) Ruskin became very angry indeed:

> I detest railways. Your railway has cut through and spoiled some of the loveliest bits of scenery in the country.

And again:

> Now, every fool in Buxton can be in Bakewell in half an hour, and every fool in Bakewell at Buxton; which you think a lucrative process of exchange – you Fools Everywhere.

But in fact the English landscape was not ruined by railways. At certain places there may be two opinions about particular pieces of line: at Dawlish, where the Great Western runs between the town and the sea; on Ludgate Hill, where a bridge is set in the foreground of the view of St Paul's cathedral from the west, though it does not block the view from Fleet Street; on the Thames at Charing Cross; near Southwark cathedral; at Conway, where the castle is shaved by the Chester & Holyhead line; or in Edinburgh, where the approach from the north and west to the best-sited station in the two kingdoms runs at the foot of Princes Street gardens. Nor did much that was historically valuable perish in the process of building the railways. It is true that what was left of Northampton castle, the castle of Berwick-on-Tweed, and St Pancras priory at Lewes disappeared; but a diversion saved Maumbury Rings at Dorchester, and a Roman pavement under the long Great Central viaduct at Leicester was preserved with special care. On balance, archaeology has gained far more from railway excavation than it has lost; and where amenities have been spoiled, it is more often (as above Miller's Dale station, on Ruskin's favourite stretch between Buxton and Bakewell) the industries and settlements that have followed rather than the railway itself which are to blame.

Even a hundred and more years ago, few voices were raised against railway builders on the grounds that natural beauties or amenities were being destroyed. There were, it is true, plenty of proprietors who used some such argument to screw more money in compensation from the companies; but when the argument had served its turn, and the money was paid, most of them continued to dwell quite happily on their ravaged domains. A few cases of pertinacious opposition, with violence, there certainly were. A well-known diehard was the Earl of Harborough, who offered strenuous and successful opposition to the line proposed for the Midland's Leicester and Peterborough railway across the grounds of his seat at Stapleford Park in Leicestershire; so for over forty years, until a more complaisant proprietor agreed to a realignment which was brought into use in 1892, Midland trains had to traverse a sharp and awkward curve at Saxby. A new Idsworth House, south of Petersfield in Hampshire, was built about a mile away from the existing mansion to get clear of the direct Portsmouth railway in the fifties.

But there was not nearly so much of this kind of thing as some modern accounts might suggest. More often the railway was cheerfully accepted as an element in the scenery. In 1842, for example, when the railway between Leicester and Derby had been open for only two years, Mr Thomas Potter wrote in his description of Charnwood Forest:

> From this point, too [the summit of Long Cliff], the trains of the Midland Counties Railway may be observed, almost uninterruptedly, from Sileby to Derby, and form a pleasing object darting across the grand panorama.

The author of Murray's *Handbook for Surrey* could write in 1865 of the view from the North Downs behind Reigate:

> The railway lines from Redhill to Dorking, from East Grinstead to Three Bridges, and from Redhill far on the way to Brighton, are visible from this point; the wreaths of white smoke that float above the deep foliage of the Weald marking the progress of the trains across the old country of the Iguanodon and the Plesiosaurus.

It seemed perfectly natural to those antiquaries, who had no special interest in the intruder. White smoke against green countryside – they liked the look of it.

George Eliot wrote on the same theme, more explicit and more imaginative:

> Our Midland plains have never lost their familiar impression and conservative spirit for me; yet at every other mile, since I first looked on them, some sign of world-wide change, some new direction of human labour, has wrought itself into what one may call the speech of the landscape ... There comes a crowd of burly navvies, with pickaxes and barrows, and while hardly a wrinkle is made in the fading mother's face, or a new curve of health in the blooming girl's, the hills are cut through, or the breaches between them spanned, we choose our level, and the white steam-pennon flies along it.

One reason for this general acceptance at the time must have been that in the years since 1760 many of the country districts in England and Scotland had already been subjected to sweeping changes in their scenery. The process of enclosure by Parliamentary act led to minor landmarks being destroyed wholesale, little woods and coppices being uprooted, and small fields thrown together into large ones, which left the land in the counties most affected looking as though it had been newly shaved. The growth of hedge timber and the healing hand of time since then have made it difficult to imagine what an upheaval there was. Turnpike roads had been driven straight (or comparatively straight) from town to town, dividing fields and properties in what seemed a ruthless manner. The road from Northampton to Kettering, for example, ran straight without turning aside to a single village for eleven miles, until it came to Broughton. Then canals had been built, sometimes straight, more often following the contours of the land round the minor hills until more important features forced them into a tunnel or on to an embankment like the Grand Junction's at Wolverton or the magnificent aqueduct across the Dee valley at Pontcysyllte in Denbighshire.

Thus the construction of the railways, plunging with great gashes across the countryside as they often did, was not something quite outside the experience of the eighteen-thirties and forties. More important, the manner of doing it was, in the formative years, worthy of great public undertakings. The works of the great engineers of that period were austere, massive, imposing. They had a kind of Roman grandeur; they did not look either cheap or vulgar. The whole railway system was something more than a commercial transaction; it was a public improvement. The buildings were always decent, sometimes imposing, sometimes romantic. The bridges and viaducts were well built, solid, sometimes elegant; the tunnel-mouths were finished to suggest classic majesty or Gothic gloom. In the early period, the journey by train was a pleasure to the eye. (Since the locomotives at that time burnt coke, not coal, danger to the eyes from smuts and cinders was, if not absent, at all events not quite so great as the pictures of persons riding in open or windowless vehicles might suggest.)

In those early days, architects strove to make their railway stations worthy – indeed, often superior – additions to the towns and villages they served, and boards of directors were sometimes under criticism for spending too much money on them. At Liverpool, the Common Council gave £2,000 towards the 'beautification' of the first Lime Street terminus building in 1836 – an example of civic improvement too rarely followed since then in Britain. Euston was the finest example of monumental grandeur in a terminus; its very size, the rich appointments of its interior, impressed the departing traveller with a sense of the solidity, the immense consequence of the London & Birmingham Railway. To the Doric of Euston corresponded Ionic at Birmingham – Curzon Street station, which later became a goods-office in a mean street; and on the way only the best was good enough for the intermediate stations. At Rugby, to indicate the collegiate nature of the place, the railway was carried across a road by a Gothic arch; and later William Tite at Carlisle and T. Penson at Shrewsbury designed station fronts in a Gothic style. It was reserved to Sir Gilbert Scott in the late sixties to produce the most Gothic of all railway stations – St Pancras, whose imposing, indeed rather alarming, front masks an interior, by the engineer W. H. Barlow, of great power and simplicity. More often, handsome porticoes in one of the classical orders fronted the street in important towns: fine Corinthian at Huddersfield; splendid works at Newcastle and Monk-wearmouth; Italianate at Chester and Dover; Elizabethan at Bristol. King's Cross, of 1851, was a remarkable essay, by Lewis Cubitt, in the functional style. *The Builder* wrote of it:

> Great plainness prevails; the architect depends wholly for effect on the largeness of some of the features, the fitness of the structure for its purpose, and a characteristic expression of that purpose.

About London Bridge, however, the architect of the 1862 frontage, Henry Currey, could find no more to say to a professional audience than this:

> I shall not attempt to describe the style of the building ... being freely treated, I leave it to the ingenuity of the Institute to find a name.

Out in the country, all sorts of jolly station buildings sprang up. Many of them have been pulled about in later years, when four tracks have been laid instead of the original two, or when growing traffic and new requirements have compelled more accommodation to be provided; thus on the Brighton line only Balcombe station building still survives intact and performing its original function. The companies' architects enjoyed themselves and built plain or fancy according to their taste and the means afforded to them. Some of the original stations and other buildings remain to show travellers today where they have passed on to the line of another constituent company: north of Rugby the Elizabethan of the wayside stations commemorates the old Trent Valley Railway; up the Evenlode valley the black timber goods-sheds are characteristic of the Oxford, Worcester & Wolverhampton; down the Great Northern line from London and across the fens and marshes to Boston and Lincoln the yellow-brick buildings with low-pitched roofs recall the so-called Italian style of the Cubitts; the transition from an English to a Scottish line through Carlisle – from the solid, lumpish appointments of the London & North Western to the more elegant Caledonian – can hardly fail to be noticed by the traveller who cares to look out of the carriage window. There is not nearly so much difference to mark the change along the road.

The styles generally mark the owners. It is indeed rare to find such sympathy for the locality as is shown in adjacent stations on the Midland main line, where the frontier of sandstone and limestone is clearly indicated by the medium brown stone of Desborough station in contrast with the pale grey of its neighbour, Glendon. There was often considerable respect for the *genius loci*, especially in the obviously romantic places. The result was unfortunate, perhaps, at Conway, where the Chester & Holyhead Railway was enjoined by a section in its Act to gothicize its tubular bridge over the river close beneath the castle walls. It was happier at Bath, where the Midland contrived a classically ordered front in the local stone, with success, and at Battle, thought by the Victorians to be a particularly medieval place, where the local architect William Tress designed a Gothic building somewhat resembling a chapel. But elsewhere the buildings were experimental, even revolutionary, like King's Cross, already mentioned; the long arcaded fronts of Derby and Chester; the somewhat gaunt train-sheds of the North Eastern and the Lancashire & Yorkshire.

But enthusiasm for the early age of railway architecture needs to be held in check. Tomlinson's ponderous history of the North Eastern Railway observes that north of the Tees and Skerne, with a very few exceptions on the Carlisle line, it was difficult in the early period to find any stations that were either commodious or attractive, certainly not in Newcastle. He cites stations without platforms, without waiting rooms, without roofs, without seats, buildings taken over from other uses without adaptation, booking offices in public houses; but even with these examples to show, Northumbria must yield the palm for economy and inefficiency to Moreton-on-Lugg, on the Shrewsbury & Hereford, where the hollow trunk of an ancient tree did duty for the station building. And – not to leave Wales out completely – there was the Taff Vale's station in the principal street of Cardiff which E. L. Ahrons was given to understand had most of the architectural features of a moderately glorified fowl-house. It is fair to add that, in time, improvements were wrought at all these places.

Here and there, a country station building with more ample accommodation than usual and some architectural pretension indicates the influence of a territorial magnate (who may even have helped, by investment or merely by failing to oppose, to get the line built). Trentham and Alton Towers, on the North Staffordshire, reflected the status of Leveson-Gower, Duke of Sutherland, and Talbot, Earl of Shrewsbury; Wolferton, the station for Sandringham, with gables and half-timbering expressed the eighteen-eightyish idea of what a great house's stable and coach-house block ought to look like; and something superior to the ordinary run of things was felt to be required, and was supplied, at both the Windsor stations. But railway architects could not concern themselves only with the fronts of stations. Commentators usually consider only the elevations of buildings; yet how vastly important, to those who use them and work in them, is the plan! King's Cross, much admired by recent critics for its appearance, was designed, like many of the earliest terminals, to deal with one train at a time on the departure side and one on the arrival, and its offices were disposed accordingly; but the limitations imposed by this arrangement soon became a weariness to travellers. Important intermediate stations like Reading and Taunton were originally single-sided, trains in either direction being brought to the only platform. These have all been rebuilt, except Cambridge, where the antique arrangement persists. The plan as well as the elevation of station buildings, and the various functions they had to serve, ought always to be borne in mind; otherwise their development is unintelligible.

Stations were not the only features of the railway scene: there were imposing things like water-towers – the original London & Birmingham one long stood at Blisworth. Cuttings sometimes needed massive retaining walls; and bridges present a great variety of treatment, from the modest but often pleasing brick arch over a roadway to a monument like Brunel's Royal Albert at Saltash, and, finest of all the early railway engineers' creations, the Britannia Bridge that massively and, as it seemed, inevitably spanned the Menai Straits. Tunnel-mouths with plain mouldings, as at Audley End in Essex, or with castellated entrances, as at Shugborough in Staffordshire, or even with ruinous outlines, such as used to exist near Bath, add their punctuation to the landscape; so above all do the viaducts, with their sweep and regularity, their repeated verticals arching or branching in to the firm horizontal of the balustrade. None of the railway viaducts is ugly, except perhaps one at Dinting Vale in Derbyshire where a later generation has ruined the original symmetry. In the Sussex Weald, where Mocatta's pavilions add a formal note to the Ouse Valley viaduct at Balcombe, or in the Midlands, where the Welland valley is crossed by the plain brickwork of Harringworth, or even in the great sweep above the town at Stockport, the railway viaduct is a dramatic affair.

Almost all of the works that have just been mentioned belong to the early period. Something bad happened to the buildings that railways put up during the fifties, and during the next two decades the new ones looked almost uniformly frightful. Then with the eighties railway building began slowly to pick up again. Two stations not far apart in Sussex, both to be seen from the same road, illustrate this turn of things: Buxted, opened in 1868, a bald, ugly brick and slate affair, may be compared with Newick & Chailey, opened by the same railway company in 1885, in a tiled cottagey style then fashionable in the south of England for lodges and similar minor buildings in the country. Market Harborough, also of 1885, is another, rather grander, specimen of this revival. Unfortunately an enormous number of existing railway buildings went up in the bad period; and the recovery when it came was not universal.

This dreariness to the eye shown by the middle period of railway architecture is, of course, partly due to the general collapse of taste; but it was also due in part to the new position of the railways themselves. They were no longer concerned to establish themselves with the public, to make a favourable impression in different ways. By the fifties the Railway, as such, was accepted, and the railways could turn to scrapping with each other. There were fights – sometimes Parliamentary, sometimes legal, occasionally physical – between the companies, intent on invading, or protecting against invasion, some particular piece of territory. Expansion, amalgamation, working agreements, and such matters of railways politics filled the minds of boards and managements.

There was, too, the constant expenditure required to operate the growing traffic with safety and without intolerable delay: more locomotives and rolling stock; equipment of passenger vehicles with continuous brakes; block signalling on all lines; widening of main lines; new marshalling yards; and all the technical improvements that experience showed to be necessary. Railways were so much taken up with their own internal affairs that they hardly had time to consider the wider social aspects of their activities as they had done in the previous era; nor did they need to. So the railway station waiting-room came to reproduce features reminding the traveller of dismal economy rather than the bright optimism with which the railways had set out on their career. It was all a relative matter. Most railways were still earning pretty well; between 1864 and 1892 the London & North Western never paid less than 6 per cent on its ordinary stock. But it seemed an inadequate return in those days, and there must be economy. No wonder that Anthony Trollope had a horror of waiting-rooms; he wrote in *The Belton Estate* about the accommodation at Taunton:

> Everything is hideous, dirty, and disagreeable; and the mind wanders away, to consider why station masters do not more frequently commit suicide.

With the mid eighteen-seventies the great age of new railway building was over. Later the railways gradually began to think of their individual prestige with the public; by 1900 they were using coloured posters and other devices of modern publicity, to stress that their service was in some way better than the other companies', or that the resorts they served were more highly favoured by nature. As part of this new outlook, the appearance of new railway buildings began to improve. Bournemouth Central in 1888, Southend (Great Eastern) in 1885, Edinburgh (Princes Street) in 1894, Harrow and Hatch End on the London & North Western in 1912 – all these stations showed a desire to please. The last main line, the Great Central from Annesley, north of Nottingham, to Marylebone, with its main stations carried out in the full flush of the Jacobean revival, closed the century with a new line of railway whose buildings were not indeed in the architectural *avant-garde*, but were certainly decent examples of good current architectural practice. It was left to the London Underground in the ninteen-thirties to take the lead in archi-tectural design, as the first main lines had done in the eighteen-thirties and forties.

Throughout the middle period, when the quality of the railways' buildings was poor, locomotives and passenger coaches continued to be well designed, brightly painted, and kept in admirable condition; but the mechanical engineers were always a law to themselves. The major civil engineering works remained generally unaffected by changes of taste. They had throughout been finished with a very creditable attention to appearance; the structures of the Settle and Carlisle line in the seventies were magnificent. In the Midlands and south of England, less pleasing materials were used – too much blue brick and heavily-riveted ironwork; but in the main the engineer's part of the work was seemly.

The railway has taken its place in the landscape with all the other artificial elements that man has put there: fields, hedges, farms, roads, canals. It has taken its place because it fits in – it rarely dominates in any view – and because, unlike the airfield which must obliterate existing features to create its shaven emptiness, the railway etches in fresh detail to the scene. It rarely jars and usually pleases.

Chapter 8
Men of the early railways

It is time to turn back from the impact of the railways on their social and physical surroundings to the men who worked and directed them. If one continues for long without coming back to the people concerned, there is a serious danger of falling into the mechanistic fallacy – of thinking that events flow on in a majestic procession of cause and effect – and forgetting that railways were devised and constructed and worked according to the decisions, wise, indifferent, or foolish as the case might be, of individual men. What is sometimes overlooked, this continues to be the case.

Where was the great army of the first railwaymen recruited from? No one has yet studied in adequate detail the origins of the 100,000 or so staff of all grades who were employed on the British railways in 1851. The answer to this question would throw much light on the way the railways developed; but for the present one can only gather a few clues here and there.

In 1851 there were still over 600 miles of line under construction in Britain, with more than 6,000 miles open. What was the labour force that drove the railways across Britain? The core was formed by the skilled specialists, the lineal successors of the 'navigators' who had cut the canals. It is hardly possible that any substantial block of men could have gone over from canal to railway construction – the interval since the great age of canal-building, which was practically over by 1810, had been too long; but their name, 'navvies', did survive, and so did a good many of their characteristics and customs.

The navvy [writes Canon Roger Lloyd] was the aristocrat, the expert ... He was paid twice as much as the labourer, and he emphasized his superiority by the colourful clothing he habitually wore. The labourers did the ordinary

digging and hewing, mostly in their own districts, while the gangs of navvies
were imported for the more difficult and dangerous parts of the work.

The best of them came from the Fens; many had come over from
Ireland, as one consequence of that astonishing rise in population which
began there about 1780; and when these met Presbyterians from
Scotland there was bloodshed. They worked in wretched conditions for
good money. The wretchedness of the living conditions endured by the
labour force employed on the construction of the Woodhead Tunnel,
between Manchester and Shefffield, provokod a full-dress inquiry and
Blue Book in 1846. The navvies could on occasion show a fierce loyalty
to a master they respected. A remarkable example of their pugnacity and
loyalty occurred during the construction of the Oxford, Worcester, &
Wolverhampton Railway in 1851; it is known to railway historians as the
Battle of Mickleton Tunnel. Here the contractor, Marchant, who had
forfeited his contract after a dispute with the company, refused to hand
over the works and plant to Peto and Betts, who were to complete the
tunnel with the rest of the line. Brunel, who was engineer to the
company, arrived with a considerable body of Great Western men to
take possession. Two magistrates and 'a large body of police armed with
cutlasses' were in attendance, and the Riot Act was read, twice. Some
delay ensued, and then Peto and Betts's men marched up in force.
Troops were ordered from Coventry to the scene; but the battle had
begun and ended before they could arrive. There was a confused affray,
in which no one was actually killed, and Marchant's men had to give
way to much superior forces. It is not clear what use a half-completed
tunnel could have been to him if he had held his ground; but the affair
showed how strong were the personal allegiances of the different forces.

The navvies were naturally regarded with awe, if not with downright
terror, by most people, and many discreditable things were believed
about them. Much remarkable evidence was given before the select
committee appointed in April 1846 to inquire into the conditions in
which railway labourers worked. One thing that this evidence reveals is
the meaning normally attached to the word 'socialism' at that time. A
chaplain was asked: 'You speak of infidel opinions. Do you believe that
many of them are socialists?' He replied: 'Most of them in practice;
though they appear to have wives, very few … are married.'

In May 1848, 188,000 men were at work on some 3,000 miles of railway line not yet open for traffic. Even though this was below the peak of 1847, and though the volume of work fell off, there remained a good deal to be done for many years to come, especially in the middle sixties. The last great railway work carried out by the old type of navvy was the construction of the Midland's Settle and Carlisle line over the fells of the West Riding and Westmorland in 1869–75.

There are many local accounts of the doings of the navvies: of their fights and fancy waistcoats, their giant strength and unvarying hostility to anything that looked like interference with their own way of life. Not much has been said of the attractive side of the scene. Yet there was one. This snapshot of railway construction was written by the doctor's daughter in the retired Middlesex village of Winchmore Hill, who had evidently learned to spot a promising scene for her sketch-book:

> The excavations were beautiful in colour, the London clay being a bright cobalt blue when first cut through, and changing with exposure to orange. There were strata of black and white flints and yellow gravel; the men's white slops and the red heaps of burnt ballast made vivid effects of light and shade and colour against the cloudless sky of that excessively hot summer. [It was 1869.] There were also dark wooden planks and shorings to add neutral tints, and when the engine came the glitter of brass and clouds of white steam were added to the landscape. On Sundays and holidays the men were, many of them, resplendent in scarlet and yellow, or blue plush waistcoats and knee-breeches.

Where did the navvies go to when the volume of new railway work ran down? Some remained with contractors and went to other jobs that called for earth-shifting: docks and reservoirs, and the other great civil engineering works that crowded into the second half of the century. Some migrated and put their skill to work on the continent of Europe or in the colonies or South America. Some others must have found their way on to the permanent staff of the home railways; for a time the tracks were maintained by contract, certainly on the Great Western and in the northeast, and probably on other lines also (a practice that was revived in places on British Railways in the 1950s). There are examples of operation by contract, as on the Leicester & Swannington in the thirties and the London, Tilbury & Southend from 1854 to 1875. When the

companies themselves assumed the responsibility for daily maintenance
and operation, they normally took over the men who had been doing
the work from the contractor.

After the constructors, the men who worked the trains: where did
they come from? Many of the porters and shunters at country stations
were recruited locally and helped to provide an outlet for the rural
population reduced to distress by the operation of the new Poor Law.
Some of the guards and station-masters were displaced coachmen.
William Chaplin, principal partner in the coaching firm of Chaplin &
Horne, used his considerable influence on the London & South
Western Railway to secure appointments on the railway for them. Many
of the police constables, who combined in themselves the functions later
divided among signalmen (still often called 'bobbies' on the railway),
ticket collectors, and permanent way inspectors, probably joined the
railway service on leaving the Navy or the Army; so did guards and other
senior traffic men. The career of one such man, my great-grandfather, is
interesting, and possibly typical except in the final stage. He was a Life
Guardsman in the escort of Queen Victoria at her coronation in 1838,
left the Army in the same year, and became a guard on the Great
Western when it was first opened from Paddington. When the Great
Northern came through to London in 1850, he transferred to it (as a
good number of G.W. men did) and was appointed station master at
Hitchin. He thereby got the local coal agency; finding that it offered him
better prospects than the G.N. did, he left the railway service in 1866.

There was one obvious source for the supply of enginemen and
mechanics to the new railways, and it was fully drawn on: the coal-pits
of Northumberland and Durham, where men had been trained in the
engine-houses. Largely by the Stephensons' influence, men from the
north-east were sought for to drive the locomotives on new railways as
they came into operation all over the kingdom; even the far-off London
& Greenwich sent to the north for drivers in 1835 and 1836. Two drivers
named Weatherburn were in charge of engines on the opening day of
the Liverpool & Manchester. George Stephenson was assisted by driver
Weatherburn on the footplate of the inaugural train on the Leicester &
Swannington in 1832. There they had a misfortune, for the engine
chimney hit the roof of Glenfield Tunnel and was knocked off, covering
the passengers with soot. Years later, in 1859, Henry Weatherburn, of

the South Eastern Railway, requested and was given a place in Westminster Abbey at Robert Stephenson's funeral on the ground that he had driven the first locomotive, the *Harvey Combe*, used on the construction of the London & Birmingham line. These men were probably brothers from Tyneside.

Many of the drivers and mechanics went with the engines from Newcastle or Lancashire to the railways which purchased them. Daniel Gooch, appointed locomotive superintendent of the Great Western in 1837, when not quite twenty-one, was a Tynesider, and no doubt many of his first drivers were also. The first artificers at country places like Swindon and Wolverton, when engineering works were set up there, had come from the north. There are, however, no indications of a Scottish element. These new towns soon recruited from round about and formed new, close communities of a distinctive character. The 'railway towns' were in their earlier years admirable examples of paternalistic rule by enlightened companies, though things went wrong later on in respect of their government and their appearance.

The clerical staff of the early railways could normally be recruited locally without difficulty. The process of 'booking' passengers for a train was at first just the same as it had been for a coach, a tedious business involving the insertion on a paper form and its counterfoil (which remained at the issuing office and made up the 'book' referred to) of the date of issue, train time, and sometimes destination station. One Thomas Edmondson, who had been apprenticed to a cabinet-maker before he became a clerk at Brampton Junction, then called Milton, on the Newcastle & Carlisle Railway, thought all this a great waste of time. First he invented the pasteboard ticket as we know it, printed and serially numbered in advance and kept ready in racks of tubes inside the office, and then a simple and effective press to stamp on the date at the moment of issue. There is no difference, except in detail, between Edmondson's system as he invented it in 1837 and the methods in use at the great majority of railway stations throughout the world today. Edmondson left the N. & C. to join the Manchester & Leeds, which spotted his worth, in 1839. In Manchester, with backing, he could exploit his patents. Another clerk on the Manchester & Leeds, though he came from a parsonage, was a less satisfactory member of the staff; this was Branwell Brontë, the scapegrace brother of the Haworth novelists, who worked in the offices at Sowerby Bridge and Luddendenfoot stations for a short time. On the goods side, managerial staff to organize operations at the terminals switched over in some numbers from the existing carrying houses: Pickford's certainly lost some men in this way, including two who afterwards became general managers of important railways – Henry Lambert on the Great Western and George Turner on the Midland.

There could be no common origin for the officers of the new railways; the directors or engineers chose likely-looking young men and waited to see if their choice had been wise. For the senior posts, they naturally thought of the armed services, and a number of Captains appear as railway officers: Mark Huish, formerly of the Bengal Native Infantry, on the Grand Junction and then the London & North Western; Laws and Binstead on the Lancashire & Yorkshire; O'Brien on the North Eastern; Eborall and Bruyeres on the North Western; Coddington, who had a spell as an inspector of railways for the Board of Trade, on the Caledonian. Some of the early railway rulebooks bear traces of the military approach to things. On the North Western, in 1847, the rule appears: 'Every person receiving uniform must appear on duty clean and neat'; and the station master had to make a daily inspection of his station and to ensure that all the railway servants at his station came on duty 'clean in their persons and clothes, shaved, and with their shoes brushed'. Nowadays there may not seem anything very special about these regulations, when uniformed staff are found in many occupations; but in the thirties and forties it was distinctly novel. It was a constant source of remark that the railway servants were civil and did not badger passengers for tips. Uniform clothing and good discipline had already been seen in one particularly enterprising factory in the seventeen-nineties – Matthew Boulton's Soho Mint at Birmingham; but there was nothing like it on the stage coaches and at the coach-offices, though the guards of the mail coaches were under good discipline.

Uniforms for the early Great Western traffic staff were based on the contemporary Metropolitan Police clothing, even to the 'duty-band' above the left wrist: beaver top-hat with leather crown and side-stays; rifle-green cloth tail coat and waistcoat; Oxford mixture trousers; uniform buttons. Porters wore glazed top-hats in 1838; they had green plush or corduroy uniform until 1852, when the colour was changed to brown. Enginemen and firemen apparently did not have uniform provided for them, but they were required to appear on duty dressed in white fustian clothing which was to be clean on Monday morning (or on a Sunday, if working on that day). Drivers wore hats, not caps, for many years.

For most of the men on the line the work was almost their whole life. It was frightfully uncomfortable: engines were not provided with cabs, as a usual practice, until almost the end of the century, and guards rode for years on the tops of the carriages. There was much danger in the work, most of it preventable; and it was not particularly well rewarded.

In the middle forties, engine drivers were paid about 7s. a day, on the best lines, for a six-day week, with no maximum in practice on the length of the day. Firemen got about 4s. 6d.; fitters about 5s.; labourers 3s. Pointsmen earned about 16s.–22s. a week. In comparison with other occupations at the time, these were not bad wages; but offers to trained enginemen from overseas were much more attractive, in money. Edmondson's booking-clerk job on the Newcastle & Carlisle was worth £60 a year; at the Manchester terminus he got £120. Railway provident funds seem to have begun with the Great Western one of 1838, and there were at least fifty by 1870. A superannuation fund is heard of in 1853; and various privilege facilities for travelling were secured by the staffs as the century went on. The hours were very long, and the discipline frequently harsh, even if the fines were sometimes paid into a benevolent fund. Yet the employment was fairly secure, and in that age security bred acceptance of many evils. There were a few strikes, but very few: only ten are on record in the forty years from 1830 to 1870, and none of them lasted more than two weeks – most were very short. All except one were about wages.

There were some movements towards combination among the men, and in 1865–7 there was a scurry of railway trade union activity. Though it was not successful in its immediate aims, it did lead to the foundation of an 'all-grades' railway union, as opposed to a craft union, in 1871 – the Amalgamated Society of Railway Servants. Railwaymen's wages and conditions of work first became a public issue in the nineties, but down to the end of the century it must be concluded that on the whole there was some degree of contentment. The railway unions did not wield much influence, and in the Webbs' great survey of trade unionism published in 1898 the railwaymen were hardly mentioned. They took their place in the 'Triple Alliance', with the miners and the road transport men and dockers, in the first decades of the twentieth century.

Chapter 9

Railway directors, managers and shareholders

We do not know very much about the origins of the operating staffs of the railways; but it is easier to get information about the directors. They were often people of some prominence, nationally or locally. Their names filled several pages of tiny type in each annual edition of *Bradshaw's Railway Manual, Shareholders' Guide, and Directory*, and 'the railway interest in Parliament' was duly tabulated – in 1872, 48 railway directors in the Lords and 124 in the Commons; in 1910, 74 in the Lords and 42 in the Commons. It would be a mistake to think, however, that they would all vote straight in favour of the railways on a controversial matter; many of them were also directors of shipping or industrial or commercial concerns as well, and their major interests might be opposed to the 'railway interest'.

Railway directors can be statistically examined and classified as territorial magnates, representatives of large blocks of invested capital, industrialists, and sometimes retired officers of the railways. Once or twice there was even a serving officer – William Cawkwell, general manager of the London & North Western since 1858, had a seat on the board from 1873 until his retirement in 1880; in practice, however, he delegated most of the daily management work. There were also two or three hereditary seats at the board, like the Duke of Sutherland's on the North Western and Sir Watkin Williams Wynn's on the Great Western. Such a classification may show various things about the preferences of the companies (more correctly, perhaps, of their chairmen) for having territorial or industrial or financial directors on their boards; but it will throw no light on the really interesting question – why did men become directors of railway companies? In the earliest days, no doubt they wanted to control what was being done with the capital they were putting up, and the Quakers and the 'Liverpool party', representing substantial blocks of capital which they respectively provided, were found on boards in numbers proportional to their investments. But when the hectic days were over, and it was clear that railways at home were going to be less of a speculation than a security, there was not the same need. Still men of standing and consequence in the world served on railway boards.

The railways gave their directors a good deal to do. The full board may not have met more than once a month, but there were normally a good many board committees, and a director might serve on half a dozen or more, all with monthly meetings. He would also represent the company at public events and at staff functions. For all this, the fee was rarely more than £500 a year, which meant little or nothing to the kind of man who was elected to the board of one of the big companies. True, he got a gold pass to hang from his watch-chain, giving him free travel and the special kind of consideration reserved for those who do not pay; but none of this was likely to be much of a bait for people like the Marquess of Salisbury or Sir Edward Grey or the great ironfounders and coal-owners and shipping magnates who filled the boardrooms. Certainly it was valuable for the manufacturers and the business men to be able to make sure that the railway on which they depended was run efficiently, and not too profitably; indeed, the North Eastern board was supposed to think of the trader first and the railway's interest second. If that was true, it was perhaps a pity that more railways were not run on that principle, for it was a very good railway. Occasionally an enthusiast would get on to a board and make the officers' lives miserable for a time: severe old G. P. Neele, superintendent of the line on the North Western throughout most of the last third of the nineteenth century, with railway service going back to 1847, had no time for directors who joined the board with the idea of improving their local train services (and even less for protégés of important personages who were put in as cadets; of one he said, 'as the result of any visit of inquiry he always returned with some clever but unsettling scheme for improving cross-country services and condemning existing ones'). There was also the economical director, who could sometimes goad a general manager into justifying his management in a full-dress reply; this happened on the North Eastern when Sir Lowthian Bell, the Cleveland ironmaster, was out for savings. Many directors had a hobbyhorse of some kind; but few accepted a seat on a board merely in order to ride it. Rather, the position was regarded as recognition of a valued career in business or in public life, in the same class as directorship of a big bank or insurance company. It was understood that those worthy of the trust ought to devote some of their time to directing the railways, much as in another way they were expected to dispense justice locally from the bench. It was part of a well-understood system of public service, which was paid for well below the market rate, and sometimes not paid for at all. On the railways the system disappeared as such at the end of 1947; but the call for unpaid public service, in transport as elsewhere, has by no means disappeared, and 'area boards' and 'consultative committees' call for the same type of public-spirited person with means somehow acquired to devote time to meetings.

The boards of the old railways were fairly large, though probably not unjustifiably so. The Great Western had sixteen directors in 1872, nineteen in 1910, twenty-three at the end; the North Western had thirty, later twenty; the South Western and the Lancashire & Yorkshire, smaller lines, got along with twelve. At the centre of affairs was the chairman, normally active in the company's affairs and attending daily at the offices; the deputy chairman sometimes likewise. The secretary was the officer specially concerned with board business – an important position, which in the early years on the Great Western, when Charles Saunders held the post, was virtually the general managership. It took a good many years for the distinction between direction and management to become understood; and even then it was not invariably kept in view. At first the directors dealt with traffic complaints themselves, if the status of the person complaining seemed to call for it. Later they were more ready to reply that such matters came under the heading of day-to-day management, and they referred the letters down.

The general manager himself, once practice had crystallized, stood at the head of the executive branch of the railway; only the secretary, solicitor, and accountant sometimes reported to the board independently of him. Committees of the board supervised the working of the different departments, with the respective officers attending to report on their affairs. But the general manager did manage, even if on some lines a strong personality at the head of the locomotive department, a Francis Webb at Crewe or a Dugald Drummond at Nine Elms, seemed to indicate pretty clearly that he ruled over a near-sovereign state whose expenses were graciously permitted to be defrayed by the rest of the railway.

Railway managers came from all kinds of employment and training in the early years; as has already been noted, many of them had been Army officers. Before long the railway service was supplying enough good material, trained 'on the job', to meet all needs at home and a good many abroad. The general manager of a big railway normally came from the traffic department; that is, from the operating and commercial side which met the public. John Aspinall, appointed to the post on the Lancashire & Yorkshire in 1899, was, exceptionally, a mechanical engineer, and both G. S. Gibb and A. Kaye Butterworth, the North Eastern's general managers from 1892 to 1921, were solicitors. But George Findlay and James Grierson, the great protagonists in the North Western and Great Western rivalry of the seventies and eighties, though both were originally civil engineers, rose on the traffic side. The railways did not need to look outside their own ranks to fill the chief executive post, and British railways were constantly providing men for high positions overseas. When the Great Eastern board in 1914 appointed Henry Thornton from Long Island to be their general manager, it was thought to be a great upheaval.

Most of the officers began their railway careers straight from school. It was not often a public school; and a university man was very rare indeed in the railway service. Sir George Findlay's career will serve to show beginnings that were not exceptional, though of course few concluded with a general managership. Findlay's father, also named George, a builder of Glasgow origin, was a masonry inspector under the Stephensons on the Liverpool & Manchester, London & Birmingham, and Manchester & Leeds Railways. The young Findlay was born in 1829 at Rainhill in Lancashire, a place soon after made famous for locomotive trials where Stephenson's *Rocket* triumphed and persuaded the Liverpool & Manchester directors to adopt steam locomotives as their motive power. He went to the grammar school at Halifax but left at fourteen and worked at masonry on the Halifax Railway and on the Trent Valley line. After this he was employed by contracting firms, until in 1850 he was engaged under Thomas Brassey as engineer for the Shrewsbury & Hereford Railway. Brassey took an operating lease of this line on completion in 1852, and he put in Findlay, being then not quite twenty-three years old, as the manager in full charge. Ten years later Brassey's lease expired, and a new lease was taken by the North Western and Great Western jointly, the North Western agreeing to take over the young but by now experienced manager. After three years of skilful participation in the tangled business of railway politics on the Welsh border, Findlay became the North Western's goods manager at Euston, chief traffic manager (under Cawkwell) in 1874, and general manager from 1880 to 1893.

The characteristic facts about this career are that the father had a railway connexion; that it began early; and that it owed nothing to any influence except the man's own work and the impression that it made on his superiors. There were no examinations passed, no careful training courses. This was true of all industry at the time; but one characteristic of the work intensified the young officer's absorption in it. Like the Wesleyan minister, he was certain to be moved somewhere else after a short residence – as he still is. So the railway service engrossed all his interest; it was his community, much more so than the place where he happened to be living.

The work of the railway, when it is properly done, is precise, exacting, and unceasing. A railway officer does not lay down his personal and immediate responsibility when he goes home at the end of the day; it stays with him, and he may at any moment have to act on it. The work is always with him; it is a life rather than an occupation. It needs patience, consistency of attention to repetitious actions and processes, slow accumulation of experience to found judgement on, and above all what Findlay's biographer found specially characteristic of him, 'a certain element of strong, plain common sense'.

It might easily have turned out that these virtues in the railway officer could become their corresponding vices – the sluggishness of a hierarchical, rule-bound organization; and certainly that was what the later nineteenth-century critics of the railways said was the matter with their arrangements. The critics added that they were grasping as well. The managements might be shrewd, they said, but only in finding reasons for opposing any innovation. Strong, plain common sense was not what was wanted, but a dash of imagination. This, and much more like it, was urged against railway management with increasing force from the middle seventies onwards, when trade took a downward turn. The trading public, and some political influences, were generally against the railways. There was a confused, unsatisfactory series of events between 1888 and 1894, when the railways' commercial affairs were turned inside out by legislation and A. J. Mundella, President of the Board of Trade, actually talked about 'bringing the railways to their senses'. They emerged from this period with the feeling, on the whole justified, that they had been badly treated; but they had certainly failed to convince the public that they were doing their job as it should be done.

There followed a considerable livening-up in all branches of railway administration between 1895 and 1914, the zenith of the steam railway age in Great Britain, when all kinds of new ideas and new techniques of management were introduced and the railway world became more ready to look outside itself to see what might be worth adopting. Overseas, too: instead of an English railway manager going to the United States to teach, as Edward Watkin did in the seventies to reorganize the Erie line, it was to learn; when George Gibb went from the North Eastern in 1901, he went to observe administration and operating practices, especially on the Pennsylvania. But the old criticisms were still made; and perhaps they always will be so long as there are railways.

Were the old railwaymen to blame for the loss of public confidence in them, or were the boards so conservative and tight-fisted that the officers could do nothing even when they wanted to? There are few written records bearing precisely on this point that can be appealed to, and all the men concerned are long since dead, so that it is difficult to get much evidence, let alone strike a balance. In any case, generalization about 120 companies, even about the twelve major lines, is usually unwarranted. Some things are clear about individual railways. The Great Western, clinging grimly on to the obsolete broad gauge in the seventies and eighties, was certainly a poor railway from its customers' point of view: train services were slow and inconvenient; station accommodation was mostly inadequate; every claim for lost or damaged goods was contested with the utmost tenacity. Times were hard, and expenditure of every kind was severely restricted. The broad gauge was at last ripped up in 1892 (it would have been better for the Great Western to do it thirty years before), and by 1895 a great recovery was beginning. The London & North Western, on the other hand, though conservative about its rolling stock and train timings, put a good deal of money in the same decades into widenings of the line, stations reconstructions, and traffic facilities generally. Sir Richard Moon, the old chairman, resigned in 1891, and capital expenditure increased a good deal after that. The Midland put in many new traffic facilities in the eighties and nineties. On the other hand, the Great Northern held back and worked more and more traffic, passenger, mineral, and goods, over the same two tracks of its main line, so that it nearly throttled itself at the London end in consequence. All over the country, traffic was growing all the time, calling for longer and heavier trains, hauled by increasingly powerful locomotives. Seaports belonging to the railways were improved, with better dock facilities – so much so that home producers alleged that railways were showing unfair preference to foreign goods imported through their docks, or exports passing through them. Following the Midland's example without much enthusiasm, all lines improved the service offered to third-class passengers; dining cars and sleeping cars were introduced, with electric lighting on the best trains; tourist and excursion traffic was developed, and seaside villages like Bournemouth began their transformation into great watering-places. There was never stagnation; but was the pace fast enough, and did the customer, whether passenger or trader, get the service he was entitled to at a fair price?

Such questions will always be asked, and likely enough there is no answer to them. By 1900 most railways could point to a string of improvements, either directly shown in better services, or internal, technical ones without which the traffics could not have been handled. It was a marvel, indeed, how the London suburban railways managed to get their steam trains in and out of their terminal stations, or through the crowded, smoke-laden Inner Circle; it must be admitted that the passengers did not always appreciate how marvellous it all was. On the whole, with big exceptions like the Great Western before the end of the broad gauge, the lines south of the Thames, the Lancashire & Yorkshire, and some of the smaller railways – on the whole the railways did keep on progressing throughout the nineteenth century, and the officers were responsible for that. There was not always competition from neighbours to stimulate them; the North Eastern had a regional monopoly, and it was one of the best-run lines.

But there was one department in which the record of the old

companies does not shine. In matters of safety – brakes, signalling, and the like – it was always public opinion, exercised finally through the action of the Board of Trade, which forced them to adopt measures that were patently overdue. Every proposed safety appliance was opposed on the ground that a false sense of security would be imparted to the driver (or guard, or signalman) so that he would feel it less necessary to attend to his primary duty, which was to secure the safety of the train by his alertness and judgement. Some of the statements in this sense that were solemnly submitted – as, for example, against providing cabs on loco-motives – would have to be seen to be believed, if one did not sometimes hear echoes of the same kind of argument used with reference to road or industrial safety today.

The story of the efforts to get all passenger trains fitted with continuous automatic brakes is a melancholy one. At the outset there were genuine technical questions at issue about the reliability of the different brakes; but even when two automatic brakes had been proved decidedly superior, the companies dragged their feet very slowly. In the end the Board of Trade lost patience with the railways, who could not be persuaded or cajoled into making an automatic brake universal on passenger trains, and got Parliament to make it compulsory in 1889, allowing three years for the job to be completed. In this business the different companies could not agree on the most satisfactory brake, and in the event, while the majority adopted the vacuum system, an im-portant minority, including the North Eastern, Great Eastern, Brighton, and Caledonian, chose the Westinghouse compressed-air brake.

There might have been good grounds for arguing the merits of either system – indeed, the debate is not dead yet; but it seems impossible to understand the state of mind which led the railways, which had so many junctions where trains passed from one system on to another, for years not merely to fail but positively to refuse to agree on a common code of bell-signals by which signalmen communicate with each other. Two years after a serious accident in Canonbury Tunnel, caused by the Great Northern signalman at the north end misunderstanding the bell-signals sent by the North London man from the south end, a meeting of the railway superintendents was called in 1883 to draw up a uniform code; but it was faced with the following letter from Alexander Christison, of the North Eastern: 'As I could not possibly agree to any alteration of our code, I think it unnecessary to have anyone at the meeting to represent the North Eastern company.' In spite of this sort of thing, which was not confined to the North Eastern, a uniform code was in the event agreed and brought into fairly general use by the end of 1884; but the difficulty of getting this done, where no additional expense was involved but only the alteration of cherished practices, throws some light on the protracted and confusing story of the rearguard action fought by all the companies against the Board of Trade over automatic brakes, where the spending of money was involved.

The question of block signalling, on which there was a similar long-drawn-out struggle between the railways and the Board, calls for some preliminary explanation. The principal threats to the safety of moving trains on railways are derailment and collision. Derailment (a word not found in English usage before 1850, when it was naturalized from France) can be prevented by proper design and maintenance of track and vehicles, by ensuring that the track is free from external obstructions, and also of course by imposing limits of speed where these are required and successfully securing their observance. Collision with other trains or railway vehicles on the running lines is prevented by maintaining adequate intervals of space; and the signalling system exists to secure such intervals. If a space interval is to be maintained, no train must be allowed to leave a point until assurance has been obtained that the preceding train has passed – and passed complete – a point farther ahead. In the early days of railways, before the invention of the electric telegraph, there was no way of securing this assurance; so the function of the signalman (or policeman, as he was usually called then) was to hold a train until a given time after the one before. The 'time-interval' system had the obvious disadvantage that if the train in front took an undue time to clear the section concerned, there was nothing except its red tail lamp to prevent the next train running into it from the rear. But as soon as the electric telegraph had been invented, a space-interval system was made possible. The signalman must wait for a message that a train had passed the next signal box before he allowed a following train to proceed: an arrangement called the 'absolute block system' because each section, from one box to the next, was called a 'block', and it was an absolute rule on passenger running lines that there might not be more than one train at a time in the block.

This applies to double lines of railway; on single lines, which are used by trains in both directions, more stringent precautions are required to prevent collisions. But the whole safety system, double or single line, depends on the electric telegraph; and although workable absolute block systems with telegraphic box-to-box communication were developed during the fifties, most of the companies had to be perpetually jogged by the Board of Trade to get more lines 'blocked'; and finally, by the same act of 1889 which imposed the braking requirements, the Board of Trade frogmarched the laggards.

Progress with this self-evidently desirable safety measure was dreadfully slow. Time-interval working – ten minutes behind a passenger train, fifteen after a goods – lasted on the Great Western main line until the seventies, though some sections through tunnels, beginning at Box, were worked by telegraph. The London & North Western had a better record, though it had been by no means brisk in adopting absolute block – by 1884 it had all but a very few lines worked on the block, and well over ninety per cent of all its points and signals were interlocked; but the chairman, Richard Moon, never lost any chance to remark that these mechanical appliances were all inducements to inattention on the part of signalmen and drivers. On the other hand, the suburban lines south of the Thames, though their rolling stock might be the subject of regular music-hall jokes, were well in advance of their prosperous northern neighbours in respect of signalling. They had to be – their close-worked train services demanded it; but it was creditable to the London, Chatham & Dover, which was a railway admired by none, to have installed the first lock-and-block working in the world, by which the operation of the signals was interlocked with the telegraph instruments, at Cambria Junction, Brixton, in 1875, and to have carried it down the main line to Dover within a few years. This was done in spite of the opinion held by J. S. Forbes, the chairman, that it was all nonsense.

On another front we get a glimpse of energetic officers being held back by the directors. In 1876 pictorial posters were beginning to be thought about, and the North Western had a scheme submitted to them. It went to the board, who like all boards rather fancied themselves on publicity; but they 'were not disposed to embark on pictorial rivalry', and the idea was dropped. It was not that the railway was hard up; in fact, it was prosperous. In the twenty years between 1870 and 1890 the dividend on North Western ordinary stocks ('Brums') never fell below 6½ per cent; and it touched 7¾. So the restraining influence must have been the board, which knew prosperity when it saw it and could not see any virtue in increasing expenses when things were going so well.

This brings us to the shareholders. What role did they play in the formation of railway policy? In the early days they frequently did take a personal interest in the policy and the management of their railways; meetings were lively affairs, when boards were sometimes thrown out of office and investigating committees of shareholders appointed. The reports produced by these committees were often scathing. But after 1866 the old speculative spirit did not often flare up, and amalgamations led to steadier dividends. 'Investors receiving a steady 5 per cent are less likely to be active at meetings than those with a faint hope of 10 per cent and a lively fear of nothing.' In addition, railway capital became dispersed over an immense number of stockholders – not necessarily the widow and the orphan who were frequently held up as typical – and the board could always find enough proxies to carry its resolutions and approve its selections to fill up vacancies. In this the railways fore-shadowed the typical large corporation of the twentieth century. So long as the dividends were dispatched regularly, the board had nothing to worry about from the stockholders; and even when there were no dividends, there was usually little that the stockholders could do but accept the board's assurance that everything possible that could be done in their interests was being done. Only occasionally does the individual come alive to us out of the meetings of the past. The voice of Mr Seneca Hughes can be heard growling and grumbling about the Great Northern's want of economy in management; Councillor Wilson, of Accrington, made himself well known at meetings of the London, Midland & Scottish Railway until the chairman took leave of him at the final meeting in 1948. Midland shareholders received free tickets to and from Derby for their meetings, and there was a similar privilege on the Manchester, Sheffield & Lincolnshire (for a time) and some Scottish lines and a few local companies; otherwise shareholders paid like everybody else. Through most of the railway age, the shareholder was very much the sleeping partner.

Chapter 10
Capital, earnings and public control

In Britain railways generally came into being to meet a need, not to create a demand. It had to be shown that there were people and things wanting transport between the places concerned before the public would promise to subscribe money and Parliament would give authority to build; however much promoters might hope or reasonably expect that new kinds of traffic might be created, they had to argue on the basis of the demand that could be demonstrated as existing. Overseas, in underdeveloped countries, including Ireland, railways might have to be provided as matters of public policy, to open up land for development; but in Britain the thing must be a business proposition. In the north of Scotland, in Sutherland and Caithness, the great proprietors might back a railway for the good that they expected it to do to their territories; but normally the promoters had to show that the money they were asking for would be reimbursed by adequate earnings soon after the opening of the line. On the other hand, the public in general looked to Parliament to protect it from such an unscrupulous monopoly as a railway might be tempted to become.

The first railways which secured incorporating Acts of Parliament entered the world equipped with a corporation framework which they inherited from the canals. Unless the whole line of railway was going to run over a single owner's land (and there were such cases in the north-east), it was most convenient, though costly, to obtain an Act of Parliament conferring power of compulsory purchase, so as to ensure that a whole project might not be frustrated by a single landowner. The process of obtaining the Act, with all the opportunities for obstruction, lobbying, and compromise that it afforded, often resulted in long and complex documents. The Stockton & Darlington's incorporating Act, modelled on the Berwick & Kelso Railway Act of 1811, was immensely long, running to sixty-one pages of print. In brief, it authorized the formation of the company, the construction of the line and branch of railway set forth, and the conveyance of minerals and merchandise; but it did not in fact explicitly provide for the carriage of passengers. The canal precedent is seen most clearly in the list of maximum scales of tolls permitted to be charged by the company for passage along the railway. It was presumed that, while the 'way and works' would be built by the company, other persons would act as the carriers on the railway thus provided. Accordingly, certain hours of the day were laid down during which traffic might be run; and it was further provided that wagons and carriages running on the line (thus apparently letting passengers in!) were to be approved by the railway company and carry the owner's name in plain lettering. The authorized works were to be completed within five years; £82,000 might be raised in shares and £20,000 by loan.

There are several features that may now seem curious about the Act. First is the idea of a highway, intended for general use but specialized in form. The analogy with the highway sprang readily to the minds of the early legislators, though it was a misleading one. A railway is a single organism, and, while it is possible for it to be operated by different undertakers, experience quickly shows that a single operator is the best, and indeed the only practicable, arrangement, both for safety and for efficiency. The Stockton & Darlington was however worked on the 'highway' principle for several years after its opening in 1825; passengers, who were explicitly authorized to be carried in the railway's second Act of 1823, were conveyed in horse-drawn coaches belonging to several different proprietors. This method of operation works well enough on waterways; but the technical difficulties of managing railway traffic boing conveyed in vehicles belonging to outside owners, who also provided haulage, quickly became obvious, though the practice did not die out altogether at once: the last fairly extensive provision of motive power by a trader over a normal railway did not come to an end until 1859, when the Northumberland & Durham Coal Co. disposed of the engines which it had used until then to haul its own traffic over the North London Railway. Private firms' locomotives, and some trains, ran over short sections of the North Staffordshire down to the grouping of 1923, and after. Private owners' wagons survived on a large scale until 1948, but haulage was of course provided by the railway. In general, however, even from the earliest days, the railways were carriers in their own vehicles as well as toll-takers; but though the tolls were subject to statutory maximum charges, the carrying charges were not so controlled, until general railway legislation beginning in 1854 introduced new conceptions.

The other thing that is specially remarkable about the Stockton & Darlington's first Act is that, although it provided that the company should keep 'proper Books of Account', there was no guidance whatever as to what this meant; nor was there any existing body of practice on the subject. Nothing was said as to auditors, or a balance sheet being drawn up, or the shareholders' right to examine accounts. There was thus no 'accountability' to the public, or to the stockholders. Railway practice developed quite fast, and Parliament began in 1844 and 1845 to insert accounting clauses in all new railway Acts. But until the Regulation of Railways Act, 1868, was passed, which imparted a precision to published railway accounts unknown up to that date, there was a good deal of excuse for the suspicion that railway accounts were made up to mystify rather than to inform the reader. In 1850 *The Times* wrote about the finances of the leading Scottish railway:

> The Caledonian Railway Company, the work neither of lawyers, nor of old women, nor spendthrifts, but of shrewd middle-aged mercantile men, is just such a tangle as one might dream of after supping on lobster salad and champagne.

Some obscurity was deliberate, but some was the result of necessary innovation. The railways were inventing new techniques of financing, and they were running well ahead of any existing auditor's technique of control.

They had some nasty shocks. In 1852 Cornelius Stovin, the London & South Western's traffic manager, decided to stay in America rather than return and explain the shortages in his part of the company's accounts. In 1856 it came out that the Great Northern had lost something like a quarter of a million pounds by fraud in their stock transfer office; the culprit, Leopold Redpath, was transported for life, but that was cold comfort for the ordinary stockholders, who got no dividend at all in the next half-year. The great lesson was the need for regular skilled auditing instead of well-intended but ineffective checks made on behalf of the shareholders by some of themselves. The general company legislation of

1844–62 owed a great deal to the railways' experiences. The railways developed their own specialized techniques of accounting, partly under Government instruction by Acts of 1868 and 1911. The main question of principle that called for skilful decision, and still does, is what types of expenditure can properly be debited to the capital account and what should be paid for out of current revenues. Railway auditing developed into a highly skilled practice; nevertheless, some prudent companies used to carry a 'Forged Stock Transfer Reserve' on their balance sheet, just in case they had another Redpath in the office – the London, Midland & Scottish maintained such a reserve until the end in 1947.

The early accounts are so imprecise that it is very difficult to discover at all certainly what the business results of the Stockton & Darlington line were. The dividend record is known; from 2½ per cent in 1826 to 8 per cent in 1832–3 and 15 per cent in 1839–41, when the market value of the £100 shares rose to £260. But it is a surprising thing that no balance sheet whatever was published during these years, and the earliest accounts still in existence date from the 1850s. There are, however, two documents which throw light on the important question: Who put up the money? The S. & D. was always 'the Quakers' Line', with special reference to the influential Pease family of Darlington; and it was rightly so called, for Edward Pease fathered it and, though not a rich man, put money into the company just when it was most needed; so also did the Backhouses, the other Quaker businessmen of Darlington. But if it is implied that it was all local capital that put the S. & D. to work, some qualification is needed. The formal agreement of shareholders to subscribe money in 1818 showed a total of £120,900, which was a good deal more than the £82,000 actually authorized. In the list are substantial amounts from outside the locality – something like £42,000 or more than a third, of which £14,000 was in the name of Joseph Gurney, a Quaker of Norwich. This was only a paper list, it is true; but in May 1826 Joseph Pease, reporting on the railway's finance, wrote: 'As I apprehend the principal strength of our railway proprietors are now in London …' The Quakers had done it by pulling all the strings they knew, and working on all their family connexions: they had got London and Norwich money to Darlington, and all parties were, as it turned out, quite well satisfied with the arrangement. The structure of the company at the end of its first year of operation was badly out of balance: paid-up capital, £67,500; loans, £102,000, including £40,000 from Gurney and £20,000 from Richardson and Overend.

It was London money, then, on top of support in the north of England, that made it possible to open the Stockton & Darlington. So it was also with the Liverpool & Manchester. A great deal was said in speeches about the spirit of the bankers and merchants of the two towns who subscribed the money; but the facts of the matter were otherwise. Manchester was not more than lukewarm about the railway anyway, and it seems that about half the promises of capital came from outside the two places. A loan of £100,000 was made by the Exchequer. The Canterbury & Whitstable, opened in 1830, got all its share capital, about £58,000, locally, but it had to raise £38,000 by loan, certainly part from Liverpool and probably some from London. The Great Western Railway originated in Bristol – it was to be called the Bristol & London Railroad; but by December 1833 it was clear that financial support would have to be sought outside Bristol and London, where there was a separate committee. Deputations of directors accordingly went to west-country towns and to South Wales and Ireland. Charles Saunders, the London secretary, described it as 'sad, harassing work', which no doubt it must have been; but it meant that £2 million was promised by the time the Bill went to Parliament in 1835.

The normal means of raising capital for these early railway schemes was by calling up local support and inducing people, often at public meetings, to buy scrip in the proposed company. Local agents were appointed to obtain subscriptions and take deposits; and for the balance the directors used all the influence they could bring to bear on bankers to accommodate them. Detailed investigation of four Yorkshire lines of the 1830s and the Caledonian, the principal Scottish railway, show substantial amounts of capital obtained through London. Railway demands would in normal times have comparatively little effect on the central money market in London. But many railway companies were floated in times of boom – 1824–5, 1835–6, and 1844–6; then it was enough for a company to put an advertisement in a paper, and the applications came flooding in. The cumulative effect of new railway companies was to increase the pressure on the economy in those years. The commercial crisis of 1847 was freely attributed to the railway mania of 1845–6, and certainly the calls made on shares issued in those years contributed to tightness of money; but Sir John Clapham concluded that the root causes were world-wide. It is probably true, on the other hand, that the railway construction continuing after each peak of promotions mitigated the ensuing slumps considerably.

After 1850 the state of things was different. Apart from quite local schemes, like the Bridport Railway or the Caterham Railway, which were meant simply to link a town with the nearest main line and were locally promoted, there were two main sources of finance: the big railway company already in existence, which could be coaxed or threatened into supporting a scheme and putting money into it; and there was the contractor like Peto or Brassey, or Thomas Savin, David Davies, and Benjamin Piercey, who built some extraordinary lines on both sides of the Welsh border. The contractor was the chief source of finance for new railways in this period. There was an amazing boom in the early sixties, when railways were being built to places like Bishop's Castle, Newport Pagnell, and Eye, or to link Manchester and Milford, or the Midland Counties and South Wales; this last actually ran from Blisworth in Northamptonshire to a rural spot called Cockley Brake Junction, some fifteen miles away in a south-westerly direction. The usual practice, when the new line was not under the protection of a powerful neighbour which lent it money, was for the contractor who carried out the constructional work to be paid in shares at a discount, sometimes as much as fifty per cent, which he proceeded to sell on the market at a profit. This would only work during a boom, but it did work: it got most of the London, Chatham & Dover line built. But the collapse of Overend, Gurney's banking house, in 1866, brought the whole flimsy edifice down. Peto went bankrupt; so did Savin and many others; and a great many investors saw the market value of their holdings cut in half, or worse.

That was the last of the great British railway manias. After about 1870 things were different again. Almost all new railway capital was raised by the existing companies, generally by private placing, not public issue; and speculative money turned to overseas railways. The contractor as a great power moved abroad as well. At home, though competition and strife between the railways continued, it took place more sedately, in board rooms or before committees of the Houses of Parliament. The railways reigned serenely, at the height of their power in the land.

It was an imposing empire, and from time to time the public, through Parliament, sought to control the dangerous monopoly that seemed to be developing. They feared a state within the State. The old framework of toll-control inherited from the canal legislation was soon found to be inapplicable, and in two or three early cases a railway thought it prudent to accept a limitation of dividend in advance. The Liverpool & Manchester was bound by its Act not to pay more than 10 per cent. This is a provision which has excited the interest of some historians, who have suggested that the continued increase of capital during the thirties, although no extensions were built, was a device intended to get round the dividend limitation. Some contemporaries thought so, too, but it was probably a perfectly legitimate capital outlay to equip the line better for carrying the increasing traffic. The Taff Vale was limited by its 1836 Act to 7 per cent with full tolls charged or 9 per cent with three-quarter tolls. The clauses were repealed in 1840, which was just as well for the T. V. shareholders, who got 17½ per cent in 1882; this was in the exceptional class with the Maryport & Carlisle, working quietly away in north-west Cumberland, which paid 10 per cent or more every year but one from 1870 to 1882, and the Barry, the South Wales dock and railway undertaking which paid 10 per cent in its first year of operation and 9½ per cent or more through most of its life.

Most of the big lines, with one or two conspicuous exceptions, jogged along in the second half of the nineteenth century with solid dividends above the 5 per cent mark on the ordinary stock. The North Western's lowest was 4 per cent in 1858; after 36 years at 6 or over (barring the exceptional year 1893, when most lines were depressed), a fall to 5½ in 1910 seemed serious. The Great Western had some wretched years in the fifties and sixties; but from 1880 it rose above 5 per cent and stayed there pretty consistently. North Eastern consols actually paid 9¼ per cent in 1873, but this was exceptional; they paid round about 6 per cent from 1885 onwards. The Midland's lowest was in 1850 – 2 per cent; it hit 7⅜ in 1864, keeping round about the 6 mark through the seventies and falling rather short of it after that; in 1897 all the stock was converted, making the Midland apparently the most heavily capitalized of the railway companies, and straightforward comparison with other lines becomes impossible. The Great Northern, after a dizzy period with some 7 per cents down to 1873, fell away and paid around 4 per cent in the eighties and nineties. The Great Eastern paid nothing in five of the first twelve years after its formation in 1862; it got to 3 in 1890, and 3⅞ in 1899, but it never reached 4. South of the Thames, the London & South Western was at or near 6 per cent from the seventies onwards, reaching 7 in 1897. The Brighton was comparatively prosperous up to 1900, but it did not touch 6 per cent after that. The less said about the financial results of the South Eastern and the London, Chatham & Dover, the better. So too with the Sheffield, or Great Central, which twice achieved 3 per cent or more, in 1880 and 1889, and then was calamitous. The Lancashire & Yorkshire flourished most in the seventies, paying 8⅜ per cent in 1872; but from 1882 it settled down to a 4 per cent level, with a better patch from 1896 to 1899. In Scotland, the Caledonian had its ups and downs, rising to 8 in 1865, going down to 3 in 1881, up to 5⅛ in 1889 and again in 1897, but falling away to 3 in 1908 and 1909. The North British was less prosperous; 'nil' was paid for five years running, 1867 to 1871, and again in 1874. The ordinaries got nothing in 1891 and 1895, and after that they twice saw 2 per cent, in 1903 and 1904.

These figures refer to individual companies. What was the average rate of remuneration for all the capital invested in the British railways? The calculation is virtually impossible to make, because of the conversions and exchanges of stocks that were made and because of the original premiums and discounts; but, for what it is worth, it has been worked out that the average rate of interest or dividend paid on receipts from capital issued was between 4 and 4½ per cent in 1913. A few years earlier, W. M. Acworth, in the first edition of his classic *Elements of Railway Economics*, took 4 per cent as about the average English figure. It had come down over the preceding decades as working expenses grew; but 4 per cent will do as the average earning.

Dividend limitation was not a workable, or a sensible, protection for the public. Publicists and politicians thought that some other specific means of preventing monopolistic abuses must be found, and they turned to four different kinds of remedy: nationalization; competition; regulation; and publicity. Nationalization was once taken up by the government, in 1844, and then left aside for a hundred years. Competition was generally felt throughout the nineteenth century to be a most desirable thing; but in practice Parliament gave no consistent series of answers when faced with proposals involving its opposite, the policy of amalgamation. In practice, regulation by statute enforced through the Board of Trade and the court of the Railway & Canal Commission became the accepted method of control. But the most effective means of control was publicity. The conducting of so much of their business in the open, subject to challenge at all times by Parliament, press, or individuals, probably did more than anything to keep an effective check on the railways when they were monopolists.

The idea of nationalization, or state ownership, of railways is nearly as old as the public railway itself. It was, like many other things that do not come to pass for a long time, given an early airing in the House of Lords, rather surprisingly in the mouth of Lord Londonderry, who was so enormously wealthy with the proceeds of the Durham coalpits, where his family developed a sizeable private railway system of their own, that he could look with lofty equanimity on possible infringements of the rights of property. He said in 1836 that it would be an excellent thing if every railway Act provided that, after a period to allow the company to earn repayment of capital and interest, 'the railways should revert to the public'. In 1844, a committee appointed by Gladstone, President of the Board of Trade, heard evidence from Captain Laws, of the Manchester & Leeds, in favour of immediate nationalization; G. C. Glyn, the banker, chairman of the London & Birmingham, said that if a new start were being made he would be for a state system. The result was that in the Regulation of Railways Act, 1844 (better known as the Cheap Trains Act from the sections about penny-a-mile 'Parliamentary' trains) provisions were included for state purchase of all lines *sanctioned after the passage of the Act* after twenty-one years from the authorizing Act. It is remarkable that the clauses got through at all, against the united hostility of the organized railway interest. There was much amendment, and the terms were made more favourable to the companies, during the passage of the bill through the Commons; but the limiting clause, which excluded 2,300 miles already sanctioned – in effect, most of the main trunk system of the country – made compulsory acquisition of the rest impracticable. Peel's Government felt that it would be dishonourable to vary the terms on which Parliament had sanctioned the earlier lines. Opinions as to the ethics of retrospective legislation of this kind were to change as time went on.

The purchase clauses of the 1844 Act were never used, though they were considered fully by a Royal Commission in the middle sixties. The twenty-one years had just expired, and the subject was fairly lively again; Edwin Chadwick, the great centralizer and *étatiste*, and Walter Bagehot, editor of *The Economist*, both thought and frequently said that the Government should take over the railways. In 1872 the question was being considered by another select committee when Captain Tyler, speaking no doubt from a full heart after his experiences as an inspecting officer of railways at the Board of Trade, came out in effect (though not, oddly enough, so many words) for state purchase: the issue was, he said: 'Either let the railways manage the State, or let the State manage the railways.' Some business men began to support more thorough state control; and through the eighties and nineties it was chambers of commerce and bodies of that kind who kept up agitation for state purchase, without, it seems, the remotest chance of success.

As the new century approached, socialists and trade unions took over the chief part from the traders. Without having taken any initiative in the campaign, the Amalgamated Society of Railway Servants adopted nationalization as the objective of its policy in 1894; the Trades Union Congress two years later. While the supporters of state purchase disdained no argument, they shifted their main emphasis from the hope of lower rates for goods to broader considerations of social justice and so forth. But, as well as railwaymen in their unions, suburban passengers and even railway stockholders were invited to support nationalization for the benefits it would bring them personally. Winston Churchill, then a Liberal minister, said in 1906 that the Government ought to have the railways in their hands. There was lively controversy between the specialists, particularly from about 1910 to 1914, during a period of railway labour controversies and railway strikes; but somehow the cry failed to excite much of an echo. When nationalization did come, at the end of 1947, it happened without much public argument. It came then not primarily because of anything in the transport situation which made that time especially appropriate to nationalize the railways; it happened because a great change had taken place in the ideas held by the majority of people about the relations of the State to the great 'utilities' of production and service within it. Whether by that time the bare question of ownership was relevant to the problems before the railways remained to be made clear.

The exact opposite to nationalization, free competition, was supported by a powerful and popular trend of thinking during the earlier railway-building era. The arguments for competition are familiar; but the perfectly competitive market has never existed in the British, or any other, railway world, and very rarely in the world of transport at any time. The practical questions of competition which had to be resolved came up in two main forms: whether to permit lines to be built competitive with existing lines; and whether to allow competing lines to amalgamate or conclude 'working agreements' which would have the effect of reducing competition. Parliamentary authority had to be obtained for a project of either kind. Bills seeking authority to build a new railway line were referred to a committee of the House (Lords or Commons, as the case might be), and the real battle was fought out by counsel in the committee room. Hearings were sometimes immensely protracted; railway managers made or lost their reputations in the witness-box; the barristers of the Parliamentary bar earned wonderful incomes. The final test for the committee usually came down to the familiar question: 'Will it earn enough to pay for itself?' If the answer seemed likely to be 'yes', then tenderness for existing concerns which would lose traffic to the newcomer did not prevent approval being given – 'the preamble being proved', in the jargon of the lawyers. Profitability was the yardstick; and it is one that our own generation does not disdain to apply.

When proposed amalgamations were under discussion, Parliament was not very clear in its own mind, if the expression is permissible. Its practice was very changeable. Every time it reviewed the general question: 'Should railway amalgamations be encouraged?' it decided that they should not be; and yet the process of amalgamation went steadily on, with Parliamentary approval, throughout the railway age. Three times in the nineteenth century and once in the twentieth, Parliament, when faced with proposals for important railway amalgamations, appointed committees to report on the whole question: in 1846, when the London & North Western was formed; in 1852–3, when the L. & N. W. and the Midland, and the London & South Western and the London, Brighton & South Coast, applied unsuccessfully for permission to amalgamate; in 1872–3, when, with three pairs of railways seeking fusion – the L.N.W.R. and the Lancashire & Yorkshire, the Midland and the Glasgow

& South Western, the Caledonian and the North British – all the proposals were withdrawn because a joint select committee disapproved of them without actually saying so; and in 1911, two years after the Great Northern, Great Eastern, and Great Central had withdrawn their bill for a 'working union'. But in between these full-dress discussions, the North Eastern had been formed by amalgamation in 1854, producing a district monopoly which seemed, especially to the North Eastern, to work very well indeed; the Great Eastern got a similar, though far less prosperous, district monopoly by amalgamation in 1862; the Great Western absorbed the West Midland in 1863, the Bristol & Exeter in 1876, and the South Devon in 1878; and the South Eastern and the London, Chatham & Dover were allowed to form a working union in 1899. On the other hand, Parliament repeatedly refused to sanction amalgamation of various railway and dock companies in South Wales, where the evils of transport monopoly in the early days had convinced the coal trade of the advantages of competition. The final irony came when the three lines which had been forced to drop their union proposal in 1909 were forced into amalgamation by an Act passed only twelve years later. It had been decided, after all the speeches, memoranda, pamphlets, and colloquies, that 'the effects of the limited degree of competition still existing between railway companies are not necessarily to the public advantage'. So the 1911 committee had found; and it seems fairly certain that, if the war had not come in 1914 and turned railway politics inside out, some quite important steps would have been taken sooner towards the kind of grouping that was enacted in 1921. By then it was impossible to turn the clock back to 1914 – the railway equipment and the managements had been exhausted by the burdens of war time. But some concentration would have been the inevitable outcome of government policies in the immediate post-war years.

Public ownership, then, was out of the question throughout the period; competition was ineffective; so increasingly governments turned to measures of control. At first, government regulations concerned the construction of the line; then financial practices; in the seventies and eighties, safety of operation, and rates and fares; at the end of the century wages and conditions of service for the staff. The growth of regulation over railways already authorized or in operation thus reflected pretty closely the aspects of railway working that came successively under criticism, to such an extent that Parliament felt bound to legislate about them. In total, the statutory requirements laid upon railways filled a portly volume – *Bigg's Railway Acts*; and the government department requiring a return, or the inspecting officer, was never very far away.

But, in the end, public control was exercised most effectively through the inevitable publicity in which the railways had to conduct their business. This was partly due to requirements laid down by the government, but it lay more in the very nature of railways. Promotion and authorization of lines were public processes, with ample opportunities for opposition and argument; accounts were published, after 1868, in a specified form; inspecting officers' reports on accidents were published; statistical returns of all kinds were published; passenger fares had to be exhibited at each station; and after 1873 all goods rates had to be open to inspection. These were statutory requirements which made it a peculiarly difficult thing for a railway to be secretive about its affairs. Compared with the iron and steel industry, or the coal-mines, or such impressive industrial and commercial developments as the growth of the soap and chemical and tobacco combines, every scene in the railway drama was played out in a blaze of light. That is not to say that all transactions were made known or all motives revealed; but it did mean that no railway could steal a march on a competitor by buying up land privately and suddenly opening a competing line (though a new service might be obtained by negotiating for running powers over another company's line).

Disputes between railway companies were matters of public knowledge and concern. The London & North Western wished to deny the Shrewsbury & Chester the right to sell tickets on Chester station in 1849; but it could not do so without an open squabble, in full view of the public. It was an exciting scrap while it lasted, especially for the booking clerk, who was ejected from his office and had his tickets thrown out after him. The railway 'battles' of the fifties, mostly incidents where an owning company denied, by physical obstruction, right of passage to the train of a neighbour which had, or thought it had, power to run over the line, were well attended by the public, the police, and sometimes the military as well. At Wolverhampton in 1851 a breach of the peace was apprehended when the first Shrewsbury & Birmingham train attempted to run on to the North Western's Stour Valley line towards Birmingham. The mayor, 'an army of police', troops, and some hundreds of people were in attendance; there were cheers and shouts from the multitude when the S. & B. engine 'bunted against that of the London & North Western, which, being a very powerful engine, and the brakes being screwed tightly down, received but a slight shock'. The *Wolverhampton Herald* reported all this with great glee. At Nottingham in 1852 the Midland strongly objected to the arrival at their station of a train from Grantham hauled by a Great Northern engine.

> Accordingly they got a *posse* of Midland engines together, and sent them, as on an elephant hunt, to hem in the Great Northern trespasser on all sides with its own kind; and although the driver of the latter, according to an eye-witness, made a desperate effort to charge through his captors, he was of course unsuccessful and had to submit to see his locomotive borne away into imprisonment in a disused shed. The rails to this were then pulled up so as effectually to cut off escape;

and there the captive remained for seven months.

There were doings of the same sort at Burton-on-Trent, Hastings, and Havant as well. At London Road station, Manchester, in 1857, the North Western began arresting passengers who had come by what they considered the wrong route from London (that is to say, from King's Cross via Retford and Sheffield rather than from Euston) until they caught a lawyer. He was very awkward to handle, and after that the North Western desisted. Where two railways were working trains between the same stations over the same tracks, they did not always agree to allow the trains to be used in common, and the wretched passengers had to wait, or pay excess fares. Even between Croydon and Purley it was forbidden to travel in a Brighton train if you had a South Eastern ticket for the section.

None of these doings could escape notice, and they did not. These disputes were normally settled in the end in the courts of law, or by arbitration, though the railways did not always get workable settlements there. In the case of the Great Western's Tenbury and Bewdley line, on which the North Western had been granted some running rights, the arbitrator decided that one train in one direction daily and two in the other should be allowed, thus presenting the railways with a pretty technical problem. But above all it was publicity that forced the railways into sensible settlements. Other kinds of businesses might wage price wars; there might be competition in racing the tea from China or the grain from Australia; but these contests were mostly fought out of sight. The public fuss and bother aroused by similar encounters between railways was of quite another order, because they touched individual people personally. Each railway grow a character of its own in the public mind: the different companies existed, almost as of right, as institutions casting their strong shadows in the communities they served. They seemed almost persons, so strongly did their separate characters impress themselves on the public. This is how the observant editor of Murray's *Handbook for Lancashire* put it in 1880:

> The railways in Lancashire have their peculiar social features. The London & North Western is marked by its long important-looking trains of through-passengers, most of whom are evidently made up for a long journey N. or S., and look upon it as a serious matter. Preston, some time about the afternoon, is the spot where these through-trains disgorge their tenants for feeding purposes, and a lively half-hour may be spent by the spectator, who is not in a hurry to dine, watching those who are. The Lancashire and Yorkshire line is devoted to cotton and coals and cheap passengers. On the various [cotton] market days the trains are filled with spinners and manufacturers, anxiously talking over the aspects of Change and the rise or fall of half a farthing in cotton.

In south Lancashire, people associated the London & North Western with the Church and the Conservatives; the Midland with Chapel and the Liberals. The railway was a public figure, and it was watched and criticized accordingly. That was the really effective public control during the high railway age.

Chapter 11

Railways overseas: the British tradition

The railway was invented, if that term may be used, in Britain – and, more specifically, in England. In its first few decades it was spread most thickly and developed most rapidly within Britain, and until about 1870, when the pace of industrial expansion at home began to slacken, Britain was the heart and centre of railway activity throughout the world. After that time, the continental and 'colonial' nations (using the latter term in the sense of those that had great areas to open up and develop, like Canada, the United States, Russia, Argentina) plunged ahead with railway construction, and British brains and capital turned increasingly outwards and overseas to join in laying steel rails from end to end of most of the land areas of the world. Other countries have acknowledged Britain's part in various ways: in Germany, the popular account of railway history includes a photograph of *Locomotion*, engine No. I of the Stockton & Darlington Railway of 1825, with a caption wrongly asserting that it represents the first locomotive in Germany; in Buenos Aires, a little locomotive built at Leeds stands on a pedestal above a brass tablet alleging, wrongly, that it first served in the Crimean War; in Rome, a commemorative tablet to George Stephenson was unveiled in 1881. In Russia, a main railway station is called *vokzal* after a concert hall outside St Petersburg (itself named after the Vauxhall gardens in London) which was served by the first Russian railway. The word is not derived, as has often been supposed, from the London & South Western Railway's original London terminus.

These examples show that, while the world's great railway-building age fell after 1870, Britain had had a good deal to do with railway development outside her own islands in the earlier period. Rails were being rolled at Dowlais for America in 1837 and for Russia in the middle 1840s; and Lady Charlotte Guest, wife of the great ironmaster, noted in her diary for 1842 that she saw Dowlais rails at Mainz. Robert Stephenson & Co. had by 1840 supplied locomotives to Austria, Belgium, France, Germany (Prussia, Saxony, and Bavaria), Italy, Russia, and North America. Thomas Brassey was building the Paris & Rouen Railway in the early 1840s, and his navvies were astonishing the natives by the amount of work they could do and meat they could consume. He held railway contracts in Italy, Switzerland, Spain, Belgium, Holland, Denmark, Norway, Austria, India, Canada, Australia, Mauritius, Argentina, Russia, and Rumania. These were operations conducted from Britain; but some engineers transplanted themselves for good. John Haswell, a Scot, who first designed and then managed the workshops of the Austrian Südbahn at Vienna, settled there. John Hughes, who went from Ebbw Vale in 1869 to set up a rolling mill in the Don Basin, supplied rails for many Russian lines, and the town of 3,000 inhabitants round his works was named Yuzovka after him (later it became Stalino, and later still, in 1961, it became Donetsk).

Throughout this early period, however, the importance of British efforts in railways overseas lay mainly in their pioneering aspect; it was not till the 1870s, when the trickle of capital going abroad swelled to a strong current, that the quantity of effort became really significant. In the middle of the century, nearly the whole of Britain's savings went into the equipment of Britain itself with towns and railways, comparatively little being required at this time for manufacturing industry; but from 1870 to 1914 capital flowed outwards, mainly for railways, docks, and public utilities, but also to secure the full benefits of railways – to invest in land, mines, and forests and in the production of primary commodities of all sorts. Some of this capital went in more or less speculative loans to foreign governments floated on the London market; much more was by direct investment in British companies established to operate abroad. Outside the British territories, Latin America was the most important sphere of this activity, and exotic names like Antofagasta, Leopoldina, and United of Havana became commonplace on the Stock Exchange. While it lasted, some of this activity was feverish; but the scenes describing the promotion of the South Central Pacific & Mexican Railway in the pages of Trollope's *The Way We Live Now* (1875) were written in bitterness, and on the whole the investment was not ill-judged. The war of 1914 halted this great outpouring of capital from London; and the war of 1939 brought this phase of economic history to an end by 'liquidating' the assets.

It would not be practical, or useful, to attempt a survey, however rapid, of all the world's railways in an essay of this sort. But it does seem worth reviewing some of the principal features of certain railway systems overseas, because in many countries of the world the railway has had an even more important influence on national life than in Britain. This brief review will be mainly directed to three aspects of railways in the countries chosen: their beginning and physical expansion, in terms of mileage; relations with the governments concerned; and gauge.

The importance of the first aspect, inception and spread of the railway network, is clear as an indication of the period when the country 'took off' in an economic sense on a course of development, and of its most rapid expansion. Figures of railway mileage constructed at different periods and in different countries may reasonably be criticized as being altogether too crude and superficial to supply a useful measure of railway or economic activity. The mile of route is an unsatisfactory unit when it may equally well represent four tracks on a main line, electrified and carrying heavy passenger and freight traffic in an urban or industrial region, or a mile of light single track in undeveloped country carrying, say, two trains a week. To get any valid comparison between the railway systems of the world at their different stages of development, some much more sophisticated derived statistics would have to be worked out, involving the complete track mileage (not merely the mileage of route), the freight tonnage handled, the area of the country, and its population. It would be an interesting exercise to produce an index of the economic importance of the world's different railways in some such way; but for the purpose of this essay the result would not throw much more light on the story for readers who already know that Britain and Belgium differ from, say, Russia and Australia in several important respects.

The importance of relations with the state is obvious enough to need no further remark; but it may be asked why the technical matter of gauge is important enough to require consideration along with the other two factors. The selection of any particular gauge is, it is true, a technical matter which is not of the greatest moment when the impact of railways in the world is being looked at in a large way; but the important point is that within a given land area the same gauge shall be adhered to. The technical and economic advantages attaching to the selection of any particular gauge within a given area are, unless quite exceptional conditions exist, such as on a mountain railway, completely lost if continuous onward passage throughout the whole of the land area concerned is frustrated by the need to tranship to vehicles running on another gauge. Uniformity of gauge is cheaply bought if, on some sections, performance in speed and capacity for haulage has to be sacrificed in some degree.

In all countries where the national railway system, whether private or state-owned, has succceded in creating a network which permits, even encourages, a free flow of passengers and freight in through-running vehicles from end to end of the territory, the railway has at once become a source of economic strength to the whole nation, not merely to a locality. The expansion and development which it has made possible have in turn created fresh demands on the railway and possibly given it added prosperity. But there have been other areas, with no significant differences in their physical geography, where the railway has failed to make the contribution it could have done because there is not uniformity of gauge. It has failed only in the broadest sense, perhaps, because in all cases it has been very useful to the area it immediately serves; but still it has failed to knit together and develop adjacent territories, to exert its full potential dynamic. In Australia and in Central Africa, for example, the railway has never played the part it has done in Canada or in Russia.

It is not that the railways have been badly sited, or poorly built, or inefficiently managed: indeed, the Kenya & Uganda Railway, worked as one undertaking with the harbour of Mombasa, had the reputation for many years of being the best-run railway in the British Empire, and it could show a very good result in its 'operating ratio' – the proportion of working expenses to revenue. Though the mistake has been recognized in Australia and in Africa for many years, there has not yet emerged the will, or the ability, to carry through a formidable task of conversion to a common gauge. A technical question has turned into a political problem, with a heavy financial commitment involved.

Very broadly speaking, and subject to much qualification in detail, it may be said that there are three main railway traditions in the world: the British, extending almost, though not quite, throughout the territories at one time or another under British political influence (except Canada) and through Latin America; the Continental; and the North American. There are of course variations of practice and outlook within these broad groupings; but the three traditions show distinguishing characteristics throughout, largely independent of the climate or of the gauges employed. British practice has always been strictly conditioned by the origin of its railways, and a very substantial part of their continuing business, which lay in the short haul from the coal-mine to navigable water; a relatively flat country; and comparatively short journeys for passengers. So the railway in Britain has until now always had to provide for the small, unbraked coal wagon which can get round the sharp curves in colliery sidings and can be tipped by existing appliances at the ports. The small wagon, with a loose coupling and no brake connexions, can be shunted at a great rate in marshalling yards, and it can be used for a good many loads besides coal. The presence of the unbraked, loose-coupled freight trains on his lines has governed the British railway operator's whole approach to his problems; and until full unification in 1948 there could be little hope of changing this situation. The economist Thorstein Veblen could write in 1915 of the 'silly little bobtailed carriages used in the British goods traffic' to illustrate his argument about 'depreciation through obsolescence'. For passenger traffic, as much privacy as possible in box-like compartments suited both the short-distance traffic and the social notions of Englishmen; the corridor train came only rather late, in the 1890s. The young Henry Adams, crossing New York Bay in 1850 and finding what he described as an English railway carriage on the Camden & Amboy Railroad, exclaimed: 'This was a new world; a suggestion of exclusiveness never approached in Boston; but it was amusing.' For their locomotives British designers could rely on first-class coal, and economy was not their strongest feature. The story of continuous and automatic brakes is the shadiest chapter in British railway history; the vacuum system prevailed, for reasons that even now are not entirely clear but may have had something to do with economy of first cost, and British engineers tended to take abroad with them the practices they had learned at home. In South America, however, they found the air high up on the Andes too thin to work the vacuum brake. In signalling progress Britain had a good technical record, and the characteristic semaphore board on a post was to be seen in many parts of the world. As for the track, the permanent way itself, the British tradition was for 'bullhead', the rail that bulges at top and bottom and rests in a 'chair' which is fixed to the sleepers, whereas most other countries in the world have used 'flat-bottom', spiked straight down on to the sleepers. British practice has now changed to a more developed form of flat-bottom.

Britain's nearest neighbour, Ireland, being wholly included within the United Kingdom throughout the formative years of railways, had many features in common with British practice. English railways had important interests in Ireland; the London & North Western and the Midland owned complete systems there. Much English capital was invested in Irish railways, and British railway officers transferred to and from Irish lines. But there were two things that distinguished railways in the sister island, as the Victorians called it: a wider gauge, and government sponsorship of construction. The first railway opened in Ireland, the Dublin & Kingstown of 1834, was constructed on the standard 4 ft 8½ in. gauge. The next, the Ulster, from Belfast to Portadown, opened in 1842, was laid at 6 ft 2 ins., in conformity with a recommendation from a Royal Commission in 1836. After that the Dublin & Drogheda chose 5 ft 2 ins., which was awkward for the prospect of a through route to Belfast; and the Board of Trade, appealed to for a decision, chose 5 ft 3 ins., apparently by splitting the difference between 5 ft and 5 ft 6 ins., which were put before the Board as the minimum and maximum desirable measurements. It was an odd way to decide a gauge. The result was that all rolling stock for use in Ireland had to be built specially, there was no possibility of train-ferry working, or shipment of wagons, to and from Britain. Still, all the main-line system of Ireland was built to one gauge, which was something; and there were a good many narrow-gauge lines at the fringes.

There was no parallel in Ireland to the burst of railway construction in Britain in the forties; indeed, it was difficult to keep construction going at all. But by 1852 Dublin was connected with Belfast, Cork, and Galway: a total, with some branches, of about 700 miles. In 1865, this had grown to 1,838 miles; twenty years later it was about 2,600; and at the peak, just after the 1914 war, it was 3,442. A good deal of public money was put into the Irish railways by the Parliament at Westminster, which from the outset in the 1830s had by general consent looked on this as a special problem, in which social and political considerations were more important than the economic tests applied nearer home. In the result, Government loans and grants were made for railway and light railway building right down to 1914; and because some of the spending had been unwise, the Free State, in particular, had too much railway in 1922. Reductions have been severe, and by 1971 there were no more than 1,564 miles at work. It has even been suggested that Eire may be the first country in Western Europe to run its economy altogether without railways; but this is not declared to be the policy of the Government.

After Ireland, the railways of India were a prime concern of the British administrator and investor. Development of railways in the sub-continent began with lines from Bombay, Calcutta, and Madras opened in 1853–6, in face of a considerable opposition on the ground that India, the land of great rivers, should look to improved water communications for its future transport system. The waterways certainly presented great obstacles to railway building, and there was grave doubt whether railways could be made to pay in India. This view was held both in Britain and in India, and it did not die out quickly. But Lord Dalhousie, who had presided over the rather inadequate measures taken by the home government to regulate the Railway Mania of the middle eighteen-forties, was governor-general of India in 1850; he urged that the risk should be taken and the line from Calcutta to Rajmehal should be built. This became the nucleus of the East Indian Railway, the longest and one of the most intensively operated railways in the British Empire, now part of the Eastern Railway of India. The question of gauge was a difficult one to decide: large parts of the country were suitable for a gauge broader than the standard, others would clearly not support a broad gauge either because of topography or economic condition. Dalhousie decided in 1853 that 5 ft 6 ins. should be the Indian standard, and this was adopted for all main lines. By 1870, however, the main system linking the principal areas was within sight of completion, and Lord Mayo then recommended adoption of the metre gauge for use on branch and feeder lines. There were also districts which could not support even a metre gauge, and considerable stretches of railway at 2 ft 6 ins. or less were built. In the result, at the time of partition in 1947, there were some 20,000 miles of broad, 16,000 miles of metre, and 3,900 miles of narrow-gauge line.

Construction went ahead steadily in India from the 1850s to the first world war: 2,500 miles were built in the first ten years (by 1863), nearly 4,800 by 1870, 9,000 by 1880, 16,000 by 1890, 24,700 by 1900, 32,000 by 1910, rising to a maximum of 43,000 in 1936, before the separation of Burma. From the beginning until 1869, the construction and working of railways were left entirely to companies with some form of government guarantee. Then there was a change of policy, and during the 1870s all new lines were constructed by the direct agency of the state and with state funds. From 1880 to 1907 the operations of the state and the state-aided companies went on side by side, productive lines being leased to private enterprise, while unproductive lines were undertaken by the state. After 1907, all the major lines were purchased by the government and leased back to companies to be managed by them as agents, so that in 1920 the government owned three-quarters of the Indian railway system but operated only a fifth of it. The twenties and thirties saw progressive steps to bring the railways fully under state control, until the partition of the systems between India and Pakistan in 1947 began an entirely new chapter in their histories.

Technically the Indian railways have naturally shown strong resemblances to British practice: semaphore signals, vacuum brakes, and clean locomotive outlines indicate the same tradition. But Indian requirements and Indian practice are not just the same as are found at home, as every British railwayman who goes to India discovers in a day or two. In particular, the civil engineering works, especially the bridges, are on a scale which is virtually unknown in Britain: not only the river crossings but the mountain barriers have imposed heavy tasks on the railway builders. The crossing of the Ghats, east of Bombay, by the original main line of the Great Indian Peninsula Railway involved a sensational succession of tunnels, viaducts, and reversing sidings. This was among the finest feats of the nineteenth-century railway engineer anywhere in the world.

Economically, railway and irrigation schemes went together in raising the standard of living throughout India and removing the age-old threat of famine. Strategic railways were built only in the North-West Frontier area, after the experiences of the later seventies there; it might have been better if as much attention had been given to strategic requirements in the north-east, as the Assam campaigns of 1942–5 showed. Politically the railway first enabled India to feel its unity; but economic ties were not strong enough to withstand the demand for partition, and the railways were divided with the country. India and Pakistan have no doubt that their railways are their economic backbone, and both are modernizing them and re-equipping them in spite of the difficulty of finding adequate capital. Probably no country in the world depends more heavily on its railways, or will do so for a generation to come, than these two.

In Australia the story of railway development has been in one important respect wholly deplorable, for fatal decisions were taken when the different colonies were still subject to strong influence from Britain. From home, both Gladstone and Grey recommended the Australian colonies to adopt as standard the 4 ft 8½ in. gauge, which they held would be wide enough for the needs of newly-settled countries. New South Wales and Victoria, however, both decided to prefer the wider gauge of 5 ft 3 ins., and London consented. In 1852 and 1853, accordingly, the two colonies went ahead with their first lines, Sydney to Parramatta and Melbourne to Hobson's Bay, hundreds of miles apart but designed to present no difficulty of transhipment when the rails eventually met. But in 1854 the Sydney men, over-persuaded by their new manager from Scotland, decided to revert to 4 ft 8½ ins., and no amount of protest from Melbourne would stop them. So Victoria went on to build over 4,000 miles on the broad gauge, while New South Wales built 6,000 on standard; Queensland and Western Australia, much more sparsely settled, adopted 3 ft 6 ins.; South Australia had sizeable mileages of all three gauges; and when the Commonwealth decided to link Western Australia by rail with the east, the standard 4 ft 8½ ins. was chosen, although it connected at Kalgoorlie with 3 ft 6 ins. and at Port Augusta with 5 ft 3 ins. and 3 ft 6 ins. only – the nearest rails on the standard gauge were at Broken Hill, some 200 miles farther east. Looked at in detail, the reasons for adopting all these different gauges, if taken in isolation, can be found sensible and intelligent; but what was gained in each case has been more than outweighed by the loss to Australia. This is recognized; but though ingenious plans for conversion have been put forward, no general scheme has yet been adopted because of the great expense involved and also because of the jealousies that show no signs of being overcome. A certain number of local improvements have dealt with some pockets of non-conforming gauge in South Australia, and the standard gauge has been carried through on a new alignment from the New South Wales border to Melbourne, so as to permit through running from Sydney. Conversions have been made in Western Australia also, so that through running is now possible from Sydney to Perth. In New Zealand, by contrast, after starts in the sixties with 5ft. 3in. and 4ft. 8½in. in the South Island, the 3ft. 6in. gauge was adopted under a law of 1870.

The evils of different gauges, though they are glaring, have been mitigated in Australia by the position of all its principal cities close to the coast, so that shipping has always been in a strong position for the haulage of heavy freight. But even so, the Commonwealth and its constituents would have been much better off with one gauge – even with 3 ft 6 ins. – than with the present variety. Only once has sheer weight of traffic forced a railway to introduce a section of non-conforming gauge simply in order to secure the higher capacity that the larger gauge will supply. This has happened in Japan, where the 12,000-mile railway system is laid to the 3 ft 6 in. gauge; but the growth of traffic between Tokyo and Osaka has outstripped the capacity of the tracks. The solution has been to build a parallel, self-contained railway on 4 ft 8½ ins. But this Japanese case is unique. There are many parts of the world which might be envious of that dilemma, if not of its paradoxical solution.

The railway map of Africa shows a largely unconnected series of lines leading inland from the principal inhabited places on the coast, or forming links between navigable waters. This arises naturally from the history of European settlement on the continent. If the gauges of railway also are shown, a much more complex situation can be seen. There is a large block of 3 ft 6 in. railway in the south, running from the Cape through Rhodesia to the Congo, touching the Atlantic in South West Africa and at Lobito Bay in Angola, and the Indian Ocean at Lourenço Marques and Beira in Mozambique; from Beira Lake Nyasa is also reached on the same gauge. The origin of this network lay in two 4 ft 8½ in. lines: one of two miles from Durban to the Point opened in 1860, and another leading out of Cape Town, where trains began to run in 1862. Government ownership began at the Cape in 1873 and in Natal in 1877, and 3 ft 6 in. gauge became standard. By 1880 there were 913 miles in Cape Colony; in 1899, 2,001 miles. In 1899 the Orange Free State had

442 miles, the Transvaal 881; and the Boer republics' lines were linked with the coast at Lourenço Marques without traversing British territory. This line of communication made the South African War of 1899 possible, from the republics' point of view. At Union, in 1910, the Cape contributed 3,329 miles of railway, Transvaal 1,706 miles, Natal 1,043 miles, and the Orange Free State 994 miles. From this beginning, the South African Railways have grown to a total length of 13,439 miles.

Developments from the east coast were later, dating from the nineties, and based on the metre gauge, presumably because materials and rolling stock were obtained from India. This was used by both British and Germans for construction inland from Mombasa, Tanga, and Dar-es-Salaam. These lines, now united into East African Railways, 3,000 miles long, reach as far as the lakes; and from Albertville, on the west shore of Lake Tanganyika, another metre-gauge line connects with the navigable waters of the Congo. The Sudan Railways are a considerable network of 2,000 miles, with their origin in the wars of the eighties and nineties, built to 3 ft 6 in. gauge; and the important system in Egypt, over 3,000 miles, which dates from 1852, is standard gauge. Most of the main Tunisian, Algerian, and Moroccan lines are standard gauge; the west coast, with its unconnected railways, tends to favour 3 ft 6 ins. If Cecil Rhodes had been able to carry through his Cape-to-Cairo railway dream in the nineties, he could have run it at 3 ft 6 ins. all the way from the Cape to Kena, where the main Egyptian railways then terminated, without meeting another gauge. Today there is a large block of metre gauge in Central Africa; but the emphasis on through rail routes has shifted from north-south to east-west. Links have been proposed from Northern Nigeria via Lake Chad to El Obeid in the Sudan; within the Congo, where the two gauges nearly meet; and from South West Africa to Rhodesia. From the north, the Sahara is to be opened up by rail as well as road and air. When traffic begins to flow by rail across Africa, the evils of 'break of gauge', first brought forcefully under public notice at Gloucester in the eighteen forties, will become as evident as they are in Australia.

Chapter 12

Railways overseas: the continental tradition

The railway tradition on the continent of Europe began to diverge fairly soon from the British practices imported with many of the original lines, though in general not so sharply as the American. Traces of British influence remain, even now: trains in France and Belgium run on the left-hand line, and semaphore signals in Italy are recognizable derivatives from English patterns, whereas those in France and Germany are not. During the steam age there were always some British locomotives on the Continent, such as the handsome green-painted engines built by Beyer, Peacock & Co. of Manchester for the Netherlands Railways. A curious feature that left traces for fifty years or more was the copying of Caledonian Railway designs for Belgian engines.

But apart from these superficial points, the differences in practice are striking. Most important, the continental construction gauge – the limits above and outside the rails within which the rolling stock must be built – is much more liberal. In consequence, carriages and wagons are bigger and as a rule much heavier, and locomotives are bigger in proportion; and consequently also it became necessary quite early to fit a continuous brake, and the Continent chose a compressed-air brake. There were rarely competitive railways: either the governments built the lines according to a preconceived plan, or concessions were awarded to companies for lines to handle specific traffic routes, guaranteed from interference. The whole approach to the question of railway provision was more authoritarian than in Britain, and when the lines were opened, the passenger was checked and supervised at all the stages of the journey to a degree that astonished the English traveller. Stations, too, were usually better appointed than in Britain; in large cities they were sometimes very grand indeed. The standard gauge is the unifying factor in European railways, being used universally for main lines, outside

Russia and the Iberian peninsula. The original continental standard was 1.44 m., slightly more than 4 ft 8½ ins., which meant that, while British rolling stock could run easily on the Continent, continental stock was tight to gauge in Britain. The new continental standard is 1.435 m., almost exactly the same as 4 ft 8½ ins. For one short period, when the wartime German Reich was at its greatest extent, there were thoughts of building a new railway, the *Europabahn*, from Dunkirk to the Donetz on a broad gauge, even one of 4 metres; but that was too fantastic for the technicians who would have had to carry it out.

Progress, in terms of length of line open to traffic, was not nearly as fast on the Continent as in the British Isles. The beginnings in most countries came quite quickly: France in 1832, Belgium and Germany (Bavaria) in 1835, Austria in 1837, Italy and Holland in 1839, Switzerland in 1847, Spain in 1848. But two conditions had to be fulfilled before general development could go forward: there must be a reasonable degree of political stability, and the governments had to have a clear idea how they wanted things to develop. There had, of course, to be money, too, from somewhere. In the result, the great railway expansion period in most of Europe began in the years around 1870, when railway construction in Britain was slackening off.

The very beginnings of the railway in France, before the locomotive, lay in the coal-field of Saint-Étienne; and in 1832 the steam locomotive was first put to work, for passenger as well as freight traffic, from there to Lyon. France was thus early in the field, and Marc Séguin has an honourable place in the roll of the first locomotive engineers. But the July monarchy of Louis Philippe showed itself at its least effective in the ensuing years. A few unconnected lines were approved and built, while wide-ranging debate went on almost interminably about the shape and organization of France's future railway system: should it be built and run by companies, or the state, or what conjunction of the two? It became common ground that the state must exercise a considerable amount of control and give some financial assistance if a system of the kind that France required was to emerge. Unlike Germany, France enjoyed political unity; but the economy was slack, and there was little driving force in the country. A national railway programme was drawn up in 1842, which embodied three sensible principles: first, general partnership between the state and the companies, with an eventual right of state purchase; second, geographical control of planning by the state; third, recognition of the state's right to supervise rates and charges, impose safety precautions, and be represented on the boards of the companies. Some people in England admired the good sense of this arrangement: even the contractor Thomas Brassey, who might have been expected to value competition for the grist it brought to his mill, thought the French system resulted in greater benefits to the public than the English.

But, even though the principles were sensible, the means of putting them into effect laid down in the law produced limited results. By 1850 the French system, though laid out on paper, was still fragrnentary in fact – only 1,870 miles in operation, with many gaps, against 3,735 in disunited Germany and 6,621 in the United Kingdom. The most impressive achievement of the Second Empire was to lift this figure to over 11,000 miles in 1870; it was a solid foundation for the uprising in France's economy. A higgledy-piggledy collection of company and state-owned lines was sorted out between 1852 and 1857 and fused into six great undertakings, each operated by a company, virtually without competition, in a well-defined area with its apex in Paris and its base on the sea or the frontiers: the Nord, Est, Ouest, Paris-Lyon-Mediterranée, Paris-Orléans, and Midi (this last lying south of Bordeaux; in its later years it was worked with the P.-O.).

Thus far, the arrangements were sensible, and construction and improvement of the main lines went forward with vigour; but the government's desire, shared by the localities concerned, to develop the less forward areas of the country by means of railways that were certain to be unremunerative, for some time at any rate, led to fearful administrative complications. In 1859 arrangements were made for a state guarantee of interest on new lines in such districts, and accounting arrangements of great ingenuity were established to determine the amounts payable by the state, and, it was hoped, the surplus profits ultimately receivable by the state. The time consequently spent by clerks in working out theoretical sums in violet-coloured official ink was perhaps not as much as that devoted in English railway offices to enticing away traffic that was going by a competitor's more convenient route; but it was not of great usefulness.

The Third Republic continued the Second Empire's good work, rather more than doubling the 1870 mileage in the next twenty years in spite of the loss of some 500 miles in Alsace-Lorraine. This was roughly the same rate of growth as Germany's at the same period. The railways had been unfairly blamed as partly responsible for the military collapse of 1870, and Freycinet, under Gambetta, pushed forward an ambitious and most uneconomic building programme. New conventions between the state and the companies, made in 1883, rearranged the financial provisions, and all the companies except the Nord, always the strongest, drew on the state under the interest guarantee. The P.L.M. was the next to become financially self-supporting, followed by the Orléans, Est, and Midi. A block of unremunerative lines between Nantes, Tours, and Bordeaux had come into the state's hands in 1877, and the Ouest did likewise in 1909.

It was foreseen under the conventions that the state should in the end take over all the railways itself. Expiry was timed for the decade 1950-60, but the railways, the first of France's industries to be nationalized, were in fact taken over in 1938. So the historic names, Nord, Est, P.L.M., P.-O., disappeared, to be replaced by the rather frigid initials 'S.N.C.F.' (Some technocrats within the organization said that they stood for 'Sans Nous C'était Foutu'.) Raoul Dautry, the strong man who had brought the Etat system (the old Ouest and the state lines of the seventies) from a music-hall joke up to a high standard, became minister, and under him Robert le Besnerais from the Nord was put in charge and stamped the system with his impress. The Second World War smashed through what should have been the formative years; but that disaster has been turned to good use by the gifted and forceful railwaymen who, with massive financial support from the state, have made of the French railways a new instrument which is, from the technical point of view, probably one of the finest systems in the world today.

Belgium, with its dense population and high degree of industrial activity, was the first continental state to achieve anything like a railway system; this it owed to the careful and determined guidance of its Saxe-Coburg ruler, Leopold I. By 1848 there were over 450 miles in operation; 353 of them belonged to the state system, which had completed its original plan of a cross formed by the Ostend-Liège and Antwerp-Brussels-Mons lines, intersecting at Malines. The next period, to about 1870, was marked by a comparatively slow growth of the state lines but a switch to private enterprise with foreign capital, mainly English, on the

Grand Luxembourg Railway, and French, on the Nord-Belge. In 1870, however, the Belgian state began to take over the private systems by purchase, and its mileage rose from just under 550 to over 2,500 by 1900. The process was not completed until the 1939–45 war, when the Nord-Belge was finally included in a system with a total mileage of over 3,000, the densest in the world in relation to the country's area. Belgium has always supplied the President and secretariat of the International Railway Congress Association, which has met periodically since 1885 for exchange of information and furtherance of the techniques and arts of railway management.

Developments in Belgium's northern neighbour, Holland, were not so rapid. The first line (Amsterdam to Haarlem) was opened in 1839, but the natural obstacles presented by courses of the great inland waterways, and the commercial obstacles presented by the interests concerned with them, made progress slow. By 1860 there were only 211 miles open; the next thirty years saw the length carried to 1,628, after which the additions were comparatively trivial. National policy was at first to leave the railways in the hands of companies. The three most important were the Holland Railway, mainly a German concern, built on the 6 ft 4½ in. gauge and converted to standard in 1864–6; the Dutch Rhenish, with important British interests, originally of the same broad gauge but converted in the 1850s; and the Netherlands Central, of 1863. State railways, first authorized in 1860, were originally laid in parts of the country not served by the companies, and so could hardly form a system; from 1890 onwards, however, the companies were taken over one by one. At the Hague and Rotterdam there are still two principal stations on different lines, inherited from the former companies' lines which cannot be integrated. In the early 1920s the Dutch railway system was nothing special; but from 1926 onwards rapid electrification and a very lively management turned the system into one of the best in Europe. In 1945 it was more thoroughly devastated than any other in Western Europe, but its re-equipment since then has been a model for any aspiring railway manager to study. Its last steam locomotive was put into a museum in 1957.

There were over 38,000 miles of railway in the German Empire of 1914; only 7,000 miles had been in existence by 1860, and nearly half the total was built after 1880. Political divisions had to be cleared away before really serious development could proceed; but divided Germany had done much better in the eighteen-thirties and forties than united but indecisive France. In 1850 the traveller arriving in France from overseas at Calais, Havre, Brest, or Bordeaux could not have got through by rail to any point on the French northeastern, eastern, or southern frontiers; but a passenger from Bremen, Hamburg, or Stettin could cross Germany to Cracow or Prague, and could get to the western frontier near Cologne; only one short gap remained between the north German lines and the Bavarian system down to Munich. It was closed in 1851. Two men are generally given credit for the movement of opinion which had enabled this to be done: Fritz Harkort, a Westphalian, who wrote in the 1820s, and Friedrich List, of Leipzig, who was urging a 'general German system' as early as 1833. Already in 1828, Goethe was saying to his friend Eckermann that he had no fears that Germany would not be united; its good highways and the future railways would see to that. Treitschke could later write, with only a small degree of exaggeration (for there were no roads in many parts of Prussia in 1840): 'It is the railways which first dragged the nation from its economic stagnation; they ended what the Zollverein had only begun; with such power did they break in upon all the old habits of life, that already in the forties the aspect of Germany was completely changed.' Whatever state they lived or built railways in, the Germans believed in standardizing their practices from the first; only in Baden was there any important difference in practice about gauge, and that lasted only until 1855. An association of German Railway Administrations, including of course the Austrian ones, was formed as early as 1847. Government policies differed: the south German states generally preferred direct state ownership, but Prussia relied on private capital to build and run the railways within a strict framework of state planning and supervision.

The Prussian annexations of Hanover and Hesse-Cassel in 1866 and the foundation of the German Empire in 1871 led to great changes in railway policy. In 1873 an Imperial Railway Office was established, but it succeeded in doing little except run the railways in Alsace-Lorraine; Bavarian opposition was sufficient to thwart Prussian plans for a completely unified German system. Indeed, it was not until 1893 that standard (Middle European) time took the place of ten local time zones. In 1879 Prussia turned to acquiring the private lines wholly or partly in its own territory. In the next six years it raised its ownership from 4,000 to 13,000 miles; and by 1910 there was no important main line, except that between Lübeck and Hamburg, left in private hands. Complete amalgamation of the state systems into the Reichsbahn did not come until 1922, and even after that the Bavarian section seemed to go on its own way for some years. The high level of discipline and technical skill of the German railwaymen were demonstrated in the two wars; and main-line electrification, begun in 1911 and extended over the southern lines and the industrial areas of Saxony and Silesia between the wars, has now been extended down the Rhine and throughout all the principal main lines.

The railways of Scandinavia were comparatively late in development. Industries were established generally later than in western Europe, and the climate and the topography were not favourable. The first Danish railways, beginning with the Copenhagen-Roskilde line of 1847, were privately owned, though some state assistance was given to lines in Funen and Jutland. After 1880, when 955 miles were open, the state acquired the main trunk routes, and the total network was doubled by 1900. Many secondary lines, in all about a third of the whole mileage, were left in private hands, and a few of these are still at work. There is no main-line electrification in Denmark; steam traction has been replaced by diesel. The great water obstacles lying between their main centres forced the Danes to perfect the train-ferry; the first of a splendid fleet appeared in 1889. But two arms of the sea have now been spanned by mighty bridges: the Little Belt (1934) and the Storström (1938).

Norway's railway system began in 1854, when the line between Oslo, then called Christiania, and Eidsvoll was opened for passengers. Progress was bedevilled by disputes about the gauge to be used, and some lines were built on the 3 ft 6 in. gauge; it was an attractive proposition in a mountainous country, but a wrong choice that had to be put right later. By 1900 Norway had only half its present railway mileage; Bergen was not joined to Oslo by rail until 1907, thirty-seven years after the proposal was first made.

Though Sweden's natural features are not as hostile to railways as Norway's, the system has grown comparatively late. It began in 1856 with three short lines at Mora, Gothenburg, and Malmö. The north main line reached Boden, in Lapland, in 1894, and half the system has been built since 1890. The state built and operated the main railways from the outset; by acquiring private railways, including some important cross-country lines, it now owns ninety-five per cent of the railway in the country. Electrification, begun in 1910, has been applied to all important lines. Sweden and Norway share the operation of Scandinavia's most northerly railway, which falls down to the ice-free port of Narvik from the Swedish side. Since 1902 the assured export of iron ore throughout the winter by this route has been one of the prime facts of European economic geography, and it led to the battles of Narvik in 1940.

Switzerland got its first railway (if the mile-long ending of the Alsace Railway at Basle, built in 1844, is excluded) in 1847 between Zurich and Baden. It was not very successful, and the internal state of the country was so disturbed at the time that no further line was opened for seven years. Robert Stephenson was asked in 1849 to prepare a plan for railway development, and he did so, proposing a long dorsal line from Geneva through Lyss and Olten to Zurich and Lake Constance, with a line from Basle to Lucerne crossing at Olten, and branches to Berne and Thun and to Chur. Thus he made no proposal to cross the Alps. It was a good plan, for a start, and eventually all Stephenson's proposals were carried out; but it was a slow business. As a confederation, Switzerland had to decide whether the control of railway building should lie with the cantons or with the centre; and from 1852 to 1872 the cantons retained the power to grant concessions. Development was therefore piecemeal, and it was carried out by companies. Gradually there emerged three big companies serving the German-speaking cantons of the north, and another spread over the west. By 1870 there were only 850 miles open; the next forty years took the total to over 3,000, and changed the Swiss lines from a conglomeration of local concerns to a unified administration holding a key place in the international train workings of Europe. The national system was founded in 1902 and virtually completed in 1909, leaving outside it the mainline B.L.S. (Berne-Lötschberg-Simplon) Railway and the metre-gauge Rhaetian Railways in the Grisons, as well as purely local lines, in private hands.

The great series of Alpine tunnels has turned Switzerland into the railway cross-roads – or perhaps more aptly the turn-table – of Europe. Apart from the crossings of the Semmering and the Brenner, away to the east in Austria, the first continuous rail route through the Alps was completed in 1871, when France and Italy were joined by the Mont Cenis tunnel. This stimulated plans for a north-and-south route through the Alps of Switzerland, to link Germany with Italy. The route of the Gotthard Pass was selected. Work began in 1872, but it was 1882 before the line and tunnel were opened to traffic. The Simplon came much later, in 1906, and the third of the great Swiss railway tunnels, the Lötschberg, in 1913. Completion of the Arlberg tunnel, in Austria, in 1884, created another east-west route, later followed for a time by the Orient Express. Electrification took place over most of the Swiss main lines between 1920 and 1930, and the last steam working on the Federal Railways was in 1960. In the result, Switzerland is furnished with a spendid railway system, maintained at high technical efficiency, and even more dependent than most national systems on a peaceful international climate for any sort of prosperity.

It is not surprising that, with all the wars and political divisions that afflicted the peninsula, Italy should have been a slow starter with railways. A five-mile line was opened from Naples to Portici to 1839, eight miles from Milan to Monza in 1840, and Venice was linked by a remarkable viaduct across the lagoon to Padua and Vicenza in 1846. In that year, Camillo Cavour, still a Piedmontese private gentleman, contributed a long article on the prospects of railways in Italy to the Paris *Revue Nouvelle*: 'no country', he wrote, 'is more justified than Italy in basing the greatest hopes in the effects of the railway'. He thought its moral (by which he meant political) effects would be even more important than the material benefits. When the kingdom of united Italy was established in 1860, there were 1,365 miles of working railway, nearly 4,000 miles in 1870. From then on to 1890, growth was rapid, to 7,575 miles; then there was a falling-off to 1910, with only another 2,000 miles opened; and a late burst of cut-off (or *direttissima*) lines was pushed through in the nineteen-twenties and thirties, making good some of the earlier deviations, not all of which had been necessary on engineering or traffic grounds – politics had come in. The earliest lines were all company concessions, including two from the Pope in his temporal capacity. In the early 1860s the new Italian state organized the railways in five groups, but it had to come to the rescue of the Upper Italian and Roman systems in 1865 and take them over itself. Twenty years later, after prodigious debates, all the railways were handed back to company management; those on the mainland were handled by two networks, the Mediterranean and Adriatic, with their territories divided by the Apennine range. But in 1905 the state solution was adopted, and the new administration proceeded, after a very shaky start, to run its railway in such a way that it became the thing in the twenties to say that Mussolini had at least made the trains run to time, which had long been a dream of vocal Italian patriots. The credit was really due to Admiral Costanzo Ciano. Electrification, adopted early in the north, spread down the peninsula, and high-speed diesel and electric trains sped along the new *direttissime*.

Spain's topography is, if anything, even less inviting to the railway engineer than Italy's, and its political history equally if not more disturbed; but its railways were built almost as fast – faster, if the whole Iberian peninsula is taken together. But the Iberians made a decision of basic importance which cut them off, like the Russians at the other end of Europe, from the rising flood of international railway traffic working. In 1844 they chose a broad gauge, 5 ft 6 ins., as their standard before a mile of line was open. For a mountainous country, it was a surprising decision; perhaps it showed their feeling about what the rest of the world might do or think. Spain's first line, from Barcelona to Mataró, was opened in 1848, which was eleven years after one in a Spanish island overseas, where a stretch near Havana in Cuba had been brought into service. The state decided to use the method of concessions to companies, which were largely financed from France; but frequent state interventions in their affairs, recurrent civil wars, and high working costs meant that the companies were rarely financially sound. In 1924 the state took what was virtually a half-share in financing and managing the companies, and in 1941 the logical ending came into operation – the RENFE, or Spanish National Railway System, with 8,270 miles of line, 975 of them now electrified. Portugal's first railway dates from 1856; the state now owns some two-thirds of its 3,000-mile network, of which most was built between 1870 and 1900.

The Austrian Empire has a special place in the pre-history of railways, for a horse-railway connecting Linz with Budweis in Bohemia, ninety miles away, was opened in 1832 and later extended to the salt works at Gmunden. At the end of 1836 there were 170 miles of horse-worked public railway in use. The steam locomotive when it arrived from

England was put to work in 1837 on a new line outside Vienna from Floridsdorf to Deutsch-Wagram, which became the first portion of a through route to Moravia. It was called, according to the pleasing habit of the old empire, the Kaiser Ferdinands Nordbahn, and most of the members of the imperial house were similarly commemorated. Although companies began the building of lines north and east from Vienna, where the going was comparatively good from the railway engineer's point of view, capital was very shy, and the empire had to give more and more support. The political events of 1848 and unemployment in Vienna gave a special impetus to the building of the southern link to Styria and on to Trieste and the plain of Lombardy. The whole empire had over 900 miles open by 1850. The ascent of the Semmering pass and the summit tunnel, completed in 1854, were remarkable works, and the decision to work the line by steam locomotive depending on adhesion was bold. After that the empire swung to and fro, as successive financial and political necessities bade it, between company concessions and full state management. Between 1854 and 1873 much construction was done, largely with French capital, on the concession basis, principally in the west and south; but in the seventies the state decided to take back these concessions and resume building on its own, particularly the Arlberg line to the west, and the principal companies were nationalized by 1884. In 1901 an ambitious programme of new lines, mainly leading from outlying provinces towards Trieste, was approved, including the mountainous Tauern line, and a period of intensive construction began. An army of 70,000 men was employed at its peak. In the same period the remaining important company lines were nationalized. In the last decade before 1914 the whole system was thoroughly knit together and overhauled; even if the political empire was a ramshackle affair, its railway was very far from that, and the strategic 'inner lines' of the central powers in the war of 1914–18 were largely the Austrian railways, which enabled troops to be switched from one front to another in a way that contrasted sharply with the slow and roundabout routes open to the Entente. In 1914 the mileage of the empire was about 29,000, the third on the continent, after Germany and Russia; the treaty of Saint Germain reduced the new Austria's total to just over 3,600, and it turned its communications from a largely north-and-south axis to east-and-west.

The third of the great continental empires, Russia, got its first railway, from St Petersburg to Pavlovsk and Tsarskoe Seloe, as early as 1837, but after that it proceeded very slowly indeed. By 1850 there were some 370 miles of railway in the whole vast territory; in 1851 the 404-mile link between St Petersburg and Moscow was completed for the government by Major George Washington Whistler. Though the first line was laid to 6 ft and the original line in Russian Poland was standard gauge, a width of 5 ft was finally chosen, apparently on general technical grounds and not as a defensive measure. Between 1854 and 1884 construction went ahead with fair speed, especially between the middle sixties and 1875; it was all carried out by companies with government support and control. In 1880 the mileage was about 15,000; then there was a slackening until Count Witte introduced an ambitious construction programme in the nineties, including the great Trans-Siberian Railway to Vladivostok, 4,600 miles long. In 1900 the mileage was 31,000, more than double what it had been in 1880; by 1914 it had risen to over 40,000. The reduced territories left to the Soviet Union in 1919 included 36,560 miles of railway, a figure that was raised to 46,200 miles by 1926. By 1939, with a further vast programme including the Turkestan-Siberian and the Tashkent railways, the railway mileage of the Soviet Union was 57,500. This figure does not of course reflect the task of doubling the Trans-Siberian throughout, which had been achieved in these years. In 1939, the average gross weight of a freight train was three times that in Britain, though less than the United States figure; but the tonnage moved per mile of track was three times the U.S., and four and a half times the British figure. Since the war of 1941–5, when the railways were fearfully punished, they have been largely re-equipped, and today, with an assured heavy long-distance traffic both in passengers and freight, they may well form the best utilized railway system in the world.

China, with a tenth of the habitable land of the globe and a quarter of the human race living on it, had no more than 4,700 miles of railway by 1920, with another 2,250 miles in Manchuria. One historian has written that the story reflected 'at once the main characteristics of the Chinese official classes, and the tendency of the Far Eastern policy of foreign powers'. This is a nice way of saying that little was done. What there was owed its finance, construction, equipment, and management to British, Russian, German, French, Belgian, American, and Japanese influences;

it was all very cosmopolitan. Only one thing was common to all the major lines, apart from those under Russian influence until 1905, and that was of the greatest importance – 4 ft 8½ in. gauge. After the Japanese occupation, standards were established which ended the former variety. Sun Yat-Sen's goal of 100,000 miles of railway, proclaimed in the 1920s, is still something less than a quarter fulfilled; but the next decade may well see in China a bigger development of new railway than anywhere else in the world. Meanwhile, some of the longest and heaviest freight trains worked by steam locomotives are being hauled for great distances across China. Some electrification is being undertaken, but steam will rule for many years.

Chapter 13

Railways overseas: the North American tradition

China is a far outpost of what we have called the continental tradition of railways. The railways of Europe itself, including the British Isles and the Soviet Union, range in density from the complicated systems of the South Wales valleys and the Ruhr to the tenuous link across the steppe or the tundra; they accounted by 1939 for about 250,000 miles of line, about a third of the world's total. More than another third lay in North America, where the United States alone had 250,000 miles at work in the 1920s. As in England, 1830 was the significant year when the first public railroad was opened for traffic – the Baltimore & Ohio; and there was already under construction a line 135 miles long between Charleston and Hamburg, South Carolina.

The mere recital of the length of railways opened for traffic in the United States shows that activity was on a completely different scale from Europe, though it is right to remember that many miles of railroad in the States required at the time they were built much less material and labour than in a long-inhabited country, and there was little trouble about the acquisition of land. The record shows 2,818 miles open in the first decade, by 1840; 30,000 miles by 1860; 53,000 by 1870; 93,000 by 1880; and then in the astonishing decade of the eighties the total is taken up to 193,000 miles, with 11,500 miles built in the single year 1882 and 12,800 in 1887. This immense expansion created special problems because of the vast consumption of materials, which could not all be supplied from within the United States. In 1867 15,000 tons of rail were shipped from Britain. By 1870 there was something like a mania, and in 1871 Britain sent 515,000 tons of rail. The world production of pig-iron rose from 8,900,000 tons in 1866 to 11,100,000 in 1869 and 14,400,000 in 1872. It was not all for railways, of course; iron was just beginning to be wanted in large quantities for ships. The boom broke in the first part of the seventies, and 1875 was a poor year with only 1,711 new miles opened and no imports of rail. But the sustained activity of the eighties called again for immense production efforts, and in 1882 British export of rail to the United States amounted to 1,200,000 tons. After 1890 things slowed down, so far as new construction went; but still, over 40,000 miles were added in the decade 1900–10, and at the peak, in 1916, the total route mileage was 254,250. Behind these bare figures lies a very complex story, by no means one of simple expansion and progress. For many years the railway network of the United States was much more impressive on paper than it was in fact. Railroads had been designed and were operated to serve the individual needs of the great market cities. The maps show a fine system, but they do not reveal that many railroads in the east and south had different gauges, so that through running was impossible. In some cities the vested interest of the local transit business maintained breaks of journey, involving a transfer by road across the town; and there were a good many gaps where rivers had not been bridged. It took the war between the states in the early sixties to drive home the lesson of these deficiencies, and even then wider gauges did not disappear from the Erie Railroad (6 ft) until 1878 and from some important lines in the south (5 ft) until 1886. There remained an awkward difference of half an inch (4 ft 9 ins.–4 ft 8½ ins.) on some lines; it was not cleared away on the Louisville & Nashville until 1900, and some 'tolerances' continued even after that on the Pennsylvania.

The disturbance of Mississippi carryings in the war, and the vast new production of the Middle West, had demonstrated the need for easy and assured east-and-west communications. Extension to the Pacific seaboard, achieved by 1869, was a political fact of the first importance. Financiers moved into control and built gigantic railway empires; a book was written called *The Strategy of Great Railroads*, but the word 'strategy' had no military significance – it referred to the campaigns and *grandeurs* of men like Vanderbilt, Harriman, Jay Gould, and James J. Hill. Congress never professed for a moment to entertain the notion of state railways; there was, it is true, the United States Military Rail Road system during the war, but this was a temporary expedient. (The Alaska Railroad, 470 miles from Seward to Fairbanks, was an exception, undertaken to develop a neglected territory.) But public outcries about the monopolistic practices of the railroads, culminating in the 'Granger' movement of the seventies, led to the establishment in 1887 of the Interstate Commerce Commission which increasingly exercised control over the activities of all railroads crossing state boundaries, which meant in effect all but those of merely local importance. By 1890 the railroad network had become a system. Breaks at rivers and cities had been all but eliminated; rolling stock had been provided with standardized coupling and braking, so that it could move freely over the country; through tickets and through freight loadings made long-distance travel and shipment by rail not only feasible but attractive.

Now, in the nineteen-sixties, the United States railroads, from which the steam locomotive has disappeared, face intense competition in the air for long-distance passengers, on the highways for freight and medium-distance travellers. West of Chicago, their state is comparatively good; but in the east, they are in difficulties, left with the traffic that no other transport agency wants. Long-distance passenger traffic on almost all the lines which still handle it has been nationalized in all but name. Financial disaster has overtaken the Pennsylvania Central. The pattern of the railroads' future is hard to discern.

The United States' northern neighbour, the Dominion of Canada, owes its very inception to the promise of railway construction; its continued existence was dependent on the promise being fulfilled. Without the steel bond of a transcontinental railroad, the new country could not hope to remain united, and British Columbia extracted the promise of such a line before it would join the new dominion; so equally did the maritime provinces of the Atlantic seaboard, which lacked through overland communications to central Canada. In the eighteen-sixties it had looked as though the comparatively easy north-south communications would carry the three main divisions of the country into political association with the United States, either separately or together. The Intercolonial Railway between central Canada and the Atlantic provinces was completed in 1876; but the Pacific line languished, and British Columbia spoke of secession. Only in 1885 was the task completed. From 2,065 miles of line open in 1860 there were over 13,000 in 1890 and over 42,000 in 1930. Even the development of air transport has hardly changed the essential economic fact about Canada, that it consists of an inhabited and cultivated strip never more than 200 miles wide but 3,000 miles long, created and kept alive by two lines of railway traversing the strip from end to end. One of them, Canadian National, is state-owned; the other, Canadian Pacific, is not.

The first locomotives for use in North America were delivered from Britain about the time of the Liverpool & Manchester Railway, but practices on different sides of the Atlantic diverged almost at once, and the American railwayman of today has a good deal of difficulty in grasping the conceptions, let alone the language, of British railway operation. The reasons for this divergence are clear. Britain was a small and closely-inhabited country where manufacturers were almost crying out for increased transport; North America, apart from a few districts on the eastern seaboard, was a land of scattered small communities, where the lakes and rivers certainly afforded important means of communication but railways were needed above all to open up the country, even in advance of roads. The railways were often built before the traffic they were to carry could arrive, sometimes many years before; so they were built with all possible economy. Light rails were laid on local timber; bridges and viaducts were built of trestles, not masonry; wood, not coal, was the fuel; communications and signalling were of the most elementary kind, if indeed any were supplied at all with the small number of trains running. 'The bell, whistle, headlight, and even Isaac Dripps's cowcatcher, as warning and protective devices, were all rather essential', Professor John F. Stover has remarked. With light rails, ill-made road-beds, ferocious curvature, all to reduce the original cost, it was essential to keep the load on each axle light. Locomotives and passenger carriages alike were soon equipped with 'bogies', four-wheeled trucks under the front of the engine or at each end of the passenger car. For many years, the American cars and freight wagons ran on two bogies; the same weight would have been supported by two single axles in Britain. Robert Stephenson & Co. even supplied a bogie engine in the eighteen-thirties.

As the American railroads were extended and linked together, the primary products of the Middle West were shipped through to East Coast ports, and coal and steel were sent for thousands of miles. The average length of haul rose to a high figure. So larger freight cars, longer continuously-braked trains which were not remarshalled at intermediate points, and heavier and more powerful locomotives became characteristic of North America. The open passenger car and the open sleeper of a democratic nation were very different things from boxed-in English compartments. All in all, the American railroad was a very different thing from the European railway:

In every single item, from baggage checks to bogie trucks, American railways differ from English much as cheese does from chalk [wrote W. M. Acworth in 1891].

British railway officers visited America from time to time to see what they could learn there; but their visits led to few changes. The Caledonian and the North Eastern built some high-capacity freight wagons; but their usefulness was very limited, and they were unsuccessful in practice. Only in 1902, after George Gibb had seen American organization and management methods for himself, did an English railway seriously try them out, when he introduced on the North Eastern the general use of derived statistics, including the figure now well known but then scorned by most railway managers – 'net ton-miles per engine-working hour' – which gives an index of efficiency.

What did America contribute to the railway? Paradoxically, the shortcomings of American track and the slow speeds which were all that could be achieved in the early years meant that certain amenities for passengers had to be provided early, in most cases many years, even decades, before they were adopted in Europe. There had to be provision for people to move up and down the train during their immensely long journeys. Charles Dickens and Anthony Trollope, in the forties and sixties, reported on the American passenger car, with its vestibule, its stove, and its peripatetic conductor, as something quite outside British experience. Long vehicles, mounted on bogies, with end entrances, central gangways, and reversible seat-backs were the rule by 1840. In the same decade there were sleeping cars of a kind. The fifties saw patents taken out for all-metal cars, 'reclining' seats, and a sort of early air-conditioning. George M. Pullman's first sleeping car conversion appeared in 1859, his first true sleeper in 1865. 'Clerestory' roofs, with a raised central ridge giving better ventilation and lighting, were characteristically American, though not unknown in Europe; they lasted much longer in America. Dining cars first appeared, on the Great Western of Canada, in 1867, when Pullman produced an 'hotel car' for eating and sleeping. In 1869 George Westinghouse first fitted compressed-air brakes to a train on the Pennsylvania Railroad. In 1895 the Baltimore & Ohio installed the first main-line electrification, through the tunnel under the city of Baltimore. In the ninteen-thirties, the diesel locomotive began to change the face of railways in the United States, and experience there has been the forcing-bed for railway diesel design which the rest of the world has watched and most of the world is copying.

There are other important networks in the world not mentioned in this brief review: the Latin American, Egyptian, and New Zealand railways, to name the largest; but they do not show any markedly different features which distinguish them from the broad groups already indicated. They were either state undertakings throughout or, having been encouraged by state concessions at the outset, progressively came under state control and then ownership. The process is not quite complete in South America, where the British-owned and -managed lines in Argentina survived until the nineteen-forties, and the Antofagasta in Peru and Bolivia until 1959. At the time when the railways seemed to have marked out their place in the world pretty clearly, in 1891, W. M. Acworth wrote:

> From China to Peru – the statement is made in all literalness – the nations
> of the world have, after somewhat more than half a century's experience,
> finally decided either that their governments shall own and work their
> railways, or at least that in return for a generous measure of state support
> their railways shall accept an equally ample measure of state control. Two
> countries only are to be excepted – important exceptions without doubt,
> seeing that between them they contain half the railway mileage and half the
> railway capital of the world – the United Kingdom and the United States.
> Whether or not these two great nations will in the end follow the example
> of the rest and nationalize their railways is one of the serious problems of
> the future.

Acworth was prepared to overlook, as he was entitled to do for the purposes of that argument, the very large amount of direct and indirect assistance given by the United States authorities, both national and local, to railways. It was natural enough, in a developing country, and a complete contrast to the way railways in Britain had normally to overbear inertia, if not opposition, locally and in Parliament.

We now know half the answer to Acworth's question: the British railways have been nationalized, but not so far the properties of those in the United States. Strict public control is almost inherent in the idea of a railway, as we defined it early on, which operates in an organized political society; and control seems to lead naturally, sooner or later, to ownership. No doubt Canadian Pacific, to name no others, will continue to contradict this proposition for many years to come.

Chapter 14

Railways and wars

When the bill for the incorporation of the London & Birmingham Railway was before the House of Lords' committee in July 1832, one of the witnesses in favour was Lt-Gen. Sir J. Willoughby Gordon, Quartermaster-General of the Army. He said that railways would be of great service for the transport of troops and stores – this had already been tried out on the Liverpool & Manchester. (He admitted, though, that railways could easily be destroyed by anyone with a mischievous intent.) The same officer testified in favour of the London & Southampton two years later, together with Admiral Sir Thomas Hardy and five captains of the Royal Navy.

Though this was a striking reinforcement of the railway's arguments, the thought was not new. It had been bound to occur during the lengthy discussions about the folly or advantage of speed on rails that had been going on since a famous attack on the safety of steam traction in the *Quarterly Review* of 1825.

> We should [wrote the reviewer] as soon expect the people of Woolwich to suffer themselves to be fired off by one of Congreve's ricochet rockets as trust themselves to the mercy of such a machine going at such a rate … We will back old Father Thames against the Woolwich railway for any sum.

But the men responsible for public order and for defence were not all of that opinion.

In the disturbed state of the country at that time, when there were no proper local police forces able to deal with anything more than trifling civil emergencies, the military had to be used very often to suppress commotions. This meant that troops had to be dispersed in small units or detachments, out of touch with each other and under the immediate command of junior officers. When rioting became imminent, ill-advised things were sometimes done; and reinforcements could not be sent quickly. The Government needed speedy means of transport for troops, and in December 1806 detachments for Ireland had gone from London to Liverpool by canal boat throughout instead of marching. Relays of fresh towing horses had been held ready at each stage, and the journey had been accomplished in seven days, against fourteen or so to march the distance. But with the railway, the Government could send troops from London to Lancashire in a day; and this meant that military action would be taken deliberately, not as the accidental result of some local commander's anxiety. The bloody scuffle in St Peter's Field at Manchester which was contemptuously named 'Peterloo' took place in 1819; but there were no Peterloos in the railway era.

The Home Office, with the War Office, used the railways extensively in the Chartist upheavals of the forties. On the whole, the arrangements worked well, though both the railway managements and the authorities had a good deal to learn; for it is a curious thing that, while innumerable Thomas Atkinses travelling as private citizens manage to get themselves and their wives and families transported, fed, and watered on their journeys, which may be quite complicated, the same men when travelling as disciplined troops are found to require special facilities and considerations beyond what the ordinary traveller gets. All this was beginning to be discovered in the eighteen-forties, and the Government took the opportunity to put a clause in the Railway Regulation Act of 1842 providing that regular and police forces must be carried by railway 'at the usual hours of starting' – in other words, in ordinary trains; there was no requirement to run specials. These provisions were amplified in 1844, and there followed a long series of enactments regulating the relations of the State, in its capacity as guardian of internal and external peace, and the British railways.

Military thought in the British Isles at that period looked upon the railway primarily as a valuable adjunct in the preservation of internal order, which then seemed so precarious, and in the second place as a link in the chain of transport to overseas stations, as in the case of the Southampton railway. The idea that railways might be used in actual military operations would not easily occur to British officers; the Admiralty was concerned about the South Devon Railway's coast line between Exeter and Newton Abbot, the Cornwall Railway's bridge over the Tamar at Saltash, and the Chester & Holyhead's Britannia Bridge over the Menai Straits, but only so far as they impinged on the foreshore or might prove a hindrance to navigation. Opinion does not seem to have turned to the use of the railways in military operations until the great invasion scare of 1859, when the general question of coastal defence was linked with the novel idea of armoured trains, and a circular railway round London on which they should operate. In 1862 the War Office opposed the building of a broad-gauge line from Tavistock to Launceston because it wanted to see an 'independent' – that is, a standard-gauge – railway built from Exeter to Plymouth. The disadvantages of breaks of gauge had been recognized. In 1871 the Government took powers to take possession of the railways in wartime; a good deal of thought was being given to the strategic aspects of the country's railway network.

In Germany, however, keen minds had been busy with the subject for much longer. In 1833 Friedrich Harkort, of Wetter, on the Ruhr, urged the construction of a railway from Minden to Cologne on various grounds, including its defensive value in case of a French invasion. Official sceptics demonstrated to their own satisfaction that troops would get to their destination quicker by marching; but one C. E. Pönitz, a Saxon, published a book as early as 1842 pointing to the advantage that a German railway system would confer if France and Russia attacked at the same time.

Pönitz's book was translated into French in 1844, and some French military and parliamentary leaders discussed these matters a good deal. But they did not build so much railway as the Prussians, who were able in 1846 to concentrate a whole army corps of 12,000 men near Cracow by two lines; and some troops were moved by rail to Schleswig-Holstein in 1848–50. The railway between Venice (Mestre) and Vicenza was used for military traffic in the operations of 1848. The Austrian Empire used the railway in 1850 for a ponderous movement of 75,000 men, 8,000 horses, and 1,000 vehicles from Vienna and Hungary to the Silesian frontier; but the value of this operation seems to have been limited, to judge from the admission that the troops would have marched the distance in the same time.

These comparatively minor demonstrations did, however, go to show that the great land empires would be able to use existing lines of rail to make concentrations of troops at required points behind their frontiers in a relatively short time. The next employment of rails in war was quite different, but its lessons for the future were just as important. This was in the Crimea, where the distance of some seven miles from the harbour of Balaclava to the firing line in front of Sevastopol imposed a severer strain on the supply services of the British Army than the 1,500 miles of sea passage from England to the port. In the winter of 1854–5, active operations ceased while the army struggled with its own supply line; and to assist the line of communication, a railway track, with navvies to lay it and wagons to run along it when completed, was sent from home. This was not entirely to the liking of the senior Royal Engineer officer on the spot, Sir John Burgoyne, a Peninsular veteran, who felt very doubtful indeed whether any good would come of it; but he later very handsomely acknowledged its value.

The Balaclava Railway crept into action during March 1855. It was not much of a railway; the wagons were wretched things, brought out second-hand from construction contracts in England, and they needed to be repaired or reconstructed as soon as they arrived. It seems that these vehicles were pressed into service as ambulance wagons in the reverse direction. The trains were horse-drawn, but the gradient at one point was so steep that a cable wound by a stationary engine had to be used. Later in 1855 some small steam locomotives were sent out, and their whistles reminded the returning soldiers of home. But the line did carry, at its best period, up to 700 tons of supplies and stores a day, and in the opinion of good judges the British Army could never have played its part in the assault on Sevastopol without it.

The Balaclava Railway, quite important in itself, can now be seen to have thrown up the basic problems with regard to military railways that still in some degree have to be resolved afresh in every war. These are the perennial questions whether civilian technicians are to be employed in the construction and operation of lines under military control; how far the railway can be kept free from interference by other branches of the Army; how the loading and forwarding of vehicles can be kept under control. The British Army staff had to grapple with these problems first in the Crimea. In every war since then, it seems that the lessons painfully learned in 1855 have had to be picked up all over again: that a body of civilians, privileged by higher pay than the troops and not subject to military law, is out of place near the battlefield; that a military railway service will not work satisfactorily unless it is under the direct orders of the commander-in-chief and is not liable to be disrupted by interference from subordinate and local commanders; and that unless the firmest control over loading and unloading of vehicles is maintained, the line will be choked and will quickly become unable to make the contribution expected of it. These were slow and painful lessons. If they had been picked up more quickly, several wars would have been finished sooner.

The Italian campaign of 1859 was quite short, and this particular criticism of the railway arrangements cannot be made. But both the French and the Austrians might have done more to avoid mistakes in the planning of movement by rail. The initial concentration by the French armies, when 76,000 men and 4,450 horses went by rail from Paris to the Piedmontese frontier in ten days, was well done; but the movement of supplies during the campaign was so faulty that the French could not pursue the beaten Austrians beyond the Mincio, simply for lack of food, although they had a fully-working railway communication behind them.

It was left to the American Civil War to demonstrate to all the world that the railway had come to be a strategical factor of the first importance, and furthermore that it could on occasion have an important bearing on the tactical handling of a large battle. Until then, the railway had been an ancillary; it had assisted armies to fight where the generals had decided the battles should be fought. But now the railway junction became a military objective, as important as the mountain pass or the river crossing. Atlanta, Georgia, was one such. The war between the States also produced one real-life story of adventure on the rails that has never since been surpassed, or even approached, for excitement:

> On a drab and rainy morning [12 April 1862], twenty-one Federal soldiers, disguised as civilians and led by Captain James J. Andrews, stole the locomotive, *General*, and several cars of a northbound Western & Atlantic passenger train as it stopped for breakfast at Big Shanty, Georgia. The raiders intended to proceed up the line to Chattanooga, burning bridges and blowing up tunnels, thus rendering the road useless for a long time to come. The plan was a good one and probably would have worked successfully except for three things: the wet weather, which made arson difficult; unanticipated meetings with extra trains, which involved long explanations;

and finally, the incredible determination of W. A. Fuller, the conductor of the train from which the *General* had been stolen. For one hundred miles this bulldog of a man gave chase to the thieves, continuing at times on foot, and so closely did he press the Federals that they were able neither to damage the road seriously, nor to refuel their locomotive. At last, completely out of wood and water, the *General* was abandoned at the Tennessee state line, the Andrews party vainly attempting to escape through the woods.

It is one of the few classic railway stories; and one hopes that Buster Keaton's wonderful silent film of it will never be allowed to wear out. Happily, both the *General* and the *Texas*, on which, at mile-a-minute speeds, calling for rare skill and courage on that track, Fuller completed his chase, survived all their adventures and are still preserved.

The Congress of the United States had received a report in 1860 from Col. R. Delafield in which he called attention to the perfection which the art of war was attaining in Europe. In his opinion, the English army, as he called it, could not have performed its immense labour in the siege of Sevastopol without the railway. Nevertheless, neither the Federal nor the Confederate army was quick to organize its railways successfully; they had to learn the hard way.

Two men created the United States Military Railroads, without which it is arguable that the South might have proved unconquerable: David C. McCallum, a versatile Scot, who was a poet, church architect, and railway administrator; and Herman C. Haupt, trained at West Point and then a civil engineer. Haupt was a brilliant bridge-builder; after Lincoln had seen one of his works, he said:

> That man Haupt has built a bridge across Potomac Creek … over which loaded trains are running every hour, and, upon my word, gentlemen, there is nothing in it but beanpoles and cornstalks.

Railroads in North America were then comparatively lightly-laid affairs, without any of the solidity of the early lines in Europe; but now prodigies of improvisation were wrought to span rivers and gullies, so as to keep armies supplied up to 300 miles from their bases. Sherman's amazing campaign from Chattanooga down into Georgia was sustained only by a single line of railway passing through hostile territory, frequently interfered with by the Confederates but never put out of action for longer than a few days. Even with his railway, it needed Sherman's genius to win his decisive campaign; without the railway, he could never have begun it.

This can be put another way, and American historians have done so. The South left its attempt at secession ten years too late. In 1850, with only a few disconnected railroads at its command, the North could not have mounted those massive attacks in Tennessee and down the Mississippi that broke the South. In 1850, secession could probably have been achieved, and the map of North America might well have come to be as variously-coloured as South America's. In the sixties, the South had at first sight a favourable position. It had a seaboard and a navy and could look to supporters overseas. Its economy was separate from the North's and independent of it. There were able leaders and an immensely strong patriotic emotion to sustain its very considerable war effort. Yet in spite of all this, the railway enabled the North to bring its ultimate superiority to bear and to prevail. Separatism, in all parts of the world, might take note; power could now be wielded by determined governments over great distances with complete effectiveness.

The fighting in the Austro-Prussian War of 1866 was over so soon that the transport aspects of war, which become obvious only in a prolonged campaign, showed nothing new. Chronologically, the next employment of railways in war must be sought at Zula on the coast of the Red Sea, during the British expedition against Magdala in 1867–8. This railway was a quite unimportant affair, and taught no fresh lessons. It took four months to build some eleven miles of line, while the military operations 300 miles inland were going so well that there was a scramble to get such railway as had been laid into working order for the evacuation. The details of this melancholy story are almost comic, and English readers may pause over them for a few moments and recall how their Empire's affairs were apt to be conducted in the Victorian age. The rails were obtained secondhand from different Indian railways, of five different patterns, in odd lengths, and of different weights. Most of them were unfit for further use. The fishplates, bolts, and boltholes mostly did not fit each other. No spikes were supplied to fix the rails to the sleepers. When spikes finally came, the augers for boring holes in the sleepers had been left behind at Bombay. Six ancient locomotives were sent, but only four could be put to work. One needed new driving wheels after a week's work; the boiler tubes of the second were quite worn out; the remaining two had been at work for years on Karachi docks, and were not well adapted to the one-in-sixty gradient on the new line. The wagons had no springs, no proper buffers, and plain cast-iron axle-boxes without grease. These wore out in a fortnight; as might have been expected, there was a good deal of sand about. Their couplings broke, and the spares had been left in India. The Indian labourers sent to lay the line were quite unsuitable, and recourse had to be had to 'gangs of Chinese picked up in Bombay'. These, remarkably, 'worked well and gave no trouble'. All in all, it is surprising to hear that reports of this railway greatly impressed the future emperor Menelik; but it is recorded that some twenty years later he remained very doubtful, because of the help given by this line to the invaders, about agreeing to the construction of a railway from Djibouti up to Addis Ababa, which was eventually built by the French.

This experience may have been useful enough for the Royal Engineer officers who were to grapple with the same sort of thing at Alexandria and Suakin and beside the Nile during the Sudan campaigns, but it had no bearing on affairs in Europe. There the American war was more relevant, and it was quickly studied. The Prussian General Staff had a translation of McCallum's report on the work of the U.S. Military Railroads prepared and issued. The Franco-Prussian War of 1870–1 broke out before all the organization decided on was in fact ready, but the Prussians were able to enter the war with four sections of railway troops. The German troop concentration was generally well done; in a fortnight 350,000 men with their horses and guns were moved in 1,200 special trains to their assembly areas. But the movement of supplies quickly became chaotic; a great block of wagons lay between Cologne and Frankfurt, while the troops were short of food. There had been no control on loading and dispatch of supplies, and the lines were choked. The Germans revised many features of their military railway organization in 1872.

On the French side, there was a great deal of strife between the railway administrations and the military authorities, who claimed absolute control over the operation of the railways and then proceeded to do just those things which make it impossible to transport any traffic at all. Although the Est company performed prodigies of operation in

July and August 1870, the whole administrative and movement arrangements had been so slipshod that frightful confusion resulted. Nevertheless, the troops were transported to the frontiers, and the August battles of 1870 were fought there. It might possibly have been better for the Second Empire if its marshals had not felt bound to rush into action so precipitately, or had not been able to do so; but the railway did what was required of it.

The lessons of the Franco-Prussian War were studied with great attention, and not only in the two countries immediately concerned. The British organization in South Africa in 1899–1902 was explicitly designed with the failures of 1870 in mind. The South African campaign brought out, on its own scale, the familiar difficulties: how to deal with a friendly but highly independent civil railway administration within one's own territory; how to organize a railway service in captured hostile territory (the Orange Free State Railways were not too difficult, but almost the whole technical staff of the N.Z.A.S.M., the Netherlands South Africa Railway Co., which operated the Transvaal lines, cleared out of its own accord or was thought too unreliable to be employed by the British); whether to carry out reconstruction with troops or civilians; and, again and again, how to impress on military commanders a proper regard for the functioning of the railway. Sir Percy Girouard's final comment, tactfully put by him into some other mouth, was: 'Civil railway officials have been heard to say that attacks by the enemy on the line are not nearly so disturbing to traffic as the arrival of a friendly general with his force.'

The political and strategic importance of railways was becoming better understood, between the wars as well as while they were being fought. In the last years of the nineteenth century and the first of the twentieth, the names of three railways were constantly being talked about, not so much because they were or would be undertakings of quite remarkable character as because it was plain that if built they would have profound effects on the political maps of several important parts of the world. These railways were known as the Trans-Siberian, the Baghdad, and the Cape-to-Cairo.

At first sight, it may look as if the Trans-Siberian line was above all a military railway. Construction was begun in 1891, when tension between Russia and Japan in the Far East was increasing; the line was built during the eighteen-nineties, when Japan was assaulting China and annexing Korea, and completed, with the important qualification mentioned later, in 1900; and it was the Russian supply-line for the war of 1904–5. It was an amazing undertaking, running for 4,627 miles from Chelyabinsk in the Urals to Vladivostok on the Pacific. But the Russians' object in building it was not so much to enable them to fight a war with Japan as to consolidate their Far Eastern possessions, which had been effectively held for little more than thirty years, and to develop the whole economy of Siberia. If military preparedness against Japan had really been the principal objective of the line, Tsarist Russia would have taken more effective steps to improve its capacity in the last four years before 1904. In fact, when war broke out, the line, which at that time completed its link with the Pacific via the Chinese Eastern Railway, through Manchuria, still had a considerable break at Lake Baikal, which had to be crossed by a combined train-ferry and ice-breaker. Its total effective capacity throughout was no more than three trains each way a day. When the campaign had begun, immense efforts were made to increase this figure to twelve. Rails were laid across the frozen lake, and the Circum-Baikal Railway, round the mountainous south end of the lake, was pressed forward; but the war was decided before the railway could exert its greatest efforts. It had not been built to sustain a war; its job was to provide a stimulus to colonization, to make Siberia a slightly less intolerable place to live in, and it certainly did that.

The Baghdad Railway, in its original form of a German-controlled route eastwards from the Bosphorus across Asia Minor and north Syria to the Euphrates and the Tigris, raised serious political issues between Great Britain and Germany. If it was to terminate at Baghdad, it might possibly have been regarded as an internal Turkish affair; but running to Basra, it was getting to the head of the Persian Gulf, which the Government of India regarded as being a special preserve of their own. When its sponsors suggested that the line should run to Kuwait, well down the Gulf, then there was very great anxiety indeed. After long negotiations, an understanding was at last reached between Great Britain and Germany, and an agreement was initialled with Lichnowsky, the German Ambassador in London, in June 1914, by which the portion from Baghdad to the Gulf was to be in British hands, a solution which had been unacceptable to the Germans in 1907. Railway communication from the Mediterranean to Baghdad was eventually established under different auspices, in which Germany found no place, and completed in 1940; but by then things had changed so much that only people of an older generation could remember what all the fuss over the Baghdad Railway had been about. The important thing is that there had been a great deal of fuss about a *railway*.

The idea of a Cape-to-Cairo railway, though it remained an idea, was conceived by Cecil Rhodes at the high-watermark of later nineteenth-century British imperialism. A more genuinely 'imperial' power might have created a railway from end to end of the continent as the Russians were doing in Siberia, and for the same primary reason – by intercon-necting the isolated developments in central Africa with each other and with alternative routes to the sea, to bring out their economic possibi-lities. It was a proposal for carrying traffic not from Egypt to the Cape, but intermediately. But no British government thought, or acted, like that, and the idea remained a dream. Some people thought that, with the air route for passengers, a road, or combined road-and-river, route would be an adequate substitute for a railway. But neither will do all the things a railway does, either in intensity of service or usually in regularity, and more railways will certainly be wanted in the interior of Africa. When the political future of those regions appears more assured, more railways are likely to be built. But they will not bear much resemblance to Rhodes's great plan.

The two world wars threw up again the same basic questions of control and administration that the British Army had faced in the Crimea and South Africa, the United States in Virginia and Tennessee, and the French and German and Russian armies in their earlier conflicts. They were resolved after the fashion that experience had shown to be right, by making the railway service in the military zone a military service, but very much independent of the Army's other activities on the technical side, and by ensuring that the traffic put on rail was controlled throughout by a specialized staff (called 'Movement Control' in the British Army) which was ultimately responsible direct to the commander-in-chief and was independent of the authority of local commanders. All this could have been foreseen; but what was perhaps a paradox, and something that many experts, including even some railwaymen, had not expected, was that the value of the railway in war was if anything even greater in the age of the motor vehicle and the aircraft than it had been before. The quantity of supplies needed to nourish an army in the field increased enormously; and while aircraft and motor vehicles opened up new possibilities in the tactics, and indeed in the strategy, of operations, their successes led at once to a demand for the service that only railways can supply: that is to say, assured and regular delivery, over compara-tively long distances, of supplies in such large quantities that the armies could not only live on what they were receiving but could build up reserve stocks for their next move. Beyond a certain distance of haulage, road transport consumes almost all that it can carry; and it is of course wasteful of manpower. So, in every campaign where a railway can be made to provide transport, it is brought into use at the earliest possible moment. Some peculiar railways have been pressed into military service, through the whole gamut from the narrow-gauge Romney, Hythe & Dymchurch, the funny little railways of the Italian colonies, and the rack-railways of Syria, to the bomb-shattered standard-gauge main lines of Italy, France, and Germany. Where railways did not exist, they were often built: along the Levant coast from Haifa through Beirut to Tripoli, and from the end of the Western Desert line forward to Tobruk, with a survey made forward to Benghazi in case of need.

The effort put into military railways can be judged by the number of soldiers employed on them. As Sir James Edmonds dryly observed:

> The story of the work and growth of military transportation, that is, of railways, canals, roads and docks, in 1914–18 bears the normal imprint of British campaigns. Begun on too small a scale, with very limited resources and with no provision made for expansion, 'Transportation' was extemporized against time at immense expense; it finally became a very large branch of the British forces in France.

It did, indeed: the Railway Operating Division on the Western Front numbered 18,400, organized in 67 companies, at its peak. At the Armistice there were in all 76,000 transportation troops and 48,000 labour service men in addition engaged on work for the transportation departments (which, in military language, then excluded roads). There were also transportation units in Greece, Palestine, and Mesopotamia. On the German side, the military railways of the Western front, which meant all the main-line railways west of the old Belgian and French frontiers, employed 220,000 men by April 1918; 58,000 were troops. Another 50,000 railway troops were on the Eastern and South-Eastern fronts. The French, with the war being fought on their own territory, mobilized their railway staff at their posts. There were a few French railway troops in the field, in different numbers as required from time to time; but the main force remained with the companies, which came under military control exercised by a *Commission de Réseau* for each system. No comparable figure can therefore be cited for the French railway effort. The United States Military Rail Road Service had 69,000 men overseas.

In the Second World War, the transportation service of the Royal Engineers and the Indian and Dominion forces numbered nearly 150,000 men at its greatest expansion; and those of us who were in it could have done with many more. Mobility of warfare has not, so far, made the locomotive, the wagon, and the steel rail obsolete; rather, it has shown itself a harsh master imposing on the railwaymen ever more complex, and often dangerous, duties.

The end of the Western campaign in 1918 on the line through Mons and Sedan left unanswered one question of particular interest to the staffs: could the advance have been kept up at the rate it had been going since August?

> At the date of the Armistice [says the official history] the only reliable railheads for the Fourth Army were 50 miles, and even in the north 30 miles, behind the Armistice Line. It was no longer possible for the Armies to advance at full strength.

In the event, three of the five British armies stood fast and only two advanced into Germany.

> The growing impossibility of railway and road reconstruction keeping pace with the rapid advance of the Allies was undoubtedly an important factor in influencing the mind of General Foch when he agreed to accord an armistice.

Twenty-six years later, in 1944, Allied armies were again overrunning Belgium from the west and reconstructing their communications as they went. There was a clash of opinion that autumn, which has been freely discussed since, about where and on how wide a front the Germans should be attacked. The check at Arnhem followed, and the German counter-offensive in the Ardennes prolonged the war in the west into 1945. Not until the spring were the Allies able to make a successful entry into Germany. Perhaps that did something to confirm that Foch's appreciation in 1918 had been right.

Military railways were in action behind almost every one of the widely scattered battle areas in 1939–45, and the national railway systems were bent but not broken under the strain of greatly increased traffics, black-out precautions and hostile attacks, and labour and material shortages. The history of their efforts has not yet been written; but when it has been, it will certainly be found to confirm the sense of words written by a senior official of the British Ministry of War Transport:

> Railways justify a predominant place in the war programme. A crisis in inland transport has been an invariable occurrence in major wars since railways came into being and [has] imposed a limitation on power to strike the enemy ... In Ludendorff's words, there comes a time when locomotives are more important than guns.

A young newspaper correspondent had written in his own rhetorical style of Kitchener's River War culminating at Omdurman in 1898:

> Victory is the beautiful, bright-coloured flower. Transport is the stem without which it could never have blossomed. Yet even the military student, in his zeal to master the fascinating combinations of the actual conflict, often forgets the far more intricate complications of supply.

Winston Churchill early learnt a lesson that could never have been far from his mind as Prime Minister in time of war.

Chapter 15

The new railway age

We are left with the questions: Was there really a railway age? And, when did it end? Or, what happened to it? The outline of developments in Britain and overseas given in the preceding sections has presumably answered the first question; there *was* a railway age, when economic and political power could not be achieved by any country that had not a well-organized system of railways. A country could have railways without being powerful; but to be powerful you had to have railways. The answer to the second question is more complex, because, though the high railway age gave way to something rather different about 1914, its successor was not an age that could do without railways. Before coming to that point, however, let us look at the revolution that the railway had wrought.

The great Victorian economist Alfred Marshall wrote in 1890: 'The dominant economic fact of our own age is the development not of the manufacturing but of the transport industries.' It may have seemed a paradox, but it was true. The steam railway was the economic detonator of the nineteenth century. Its first effect was to create sharp demands in specific trades and manufactures and employments; and then, by a series of reactions, to set off innumerable further demands and help to create the means of supplying them. Its full, world-wide effect was not, of course, secured until the steamship was finally established as its ally in the last fifteen years of the century; but even while the cargo trade of the world was still entrusted to sail, the revolutionary results of the railway were already being felt.

To be fully effective, the railway revolution required mechanization, by steam power, of all kinds of manufacturing processes. Steel-making and milling are perhaps the two most obvious examples; without rapid manufacture of steel and milling of flour, supplies would never have been adequate for the mounting demands of industry and transport or for the millions of additional mouths to be fed. As a result of mechanization, there arose a demand for more and more coal. Tens of thousands of men and their families accordingly went flocking into remote places where coal was to be found. Railways mostly took them there; when they had settled, railways kept them supplied with food and carried away the product. In consequence of mechanization also, factories were increasingly congregated in large towns and cities, in the days before electric power made siting of industry more flexible; and the workpeople had to live close to the factories. Specialization was the key to success. Each district of the United Kingdom, and of other countries also, had its particular range of products: the Victorian child's card-game which showed steel and shipbuilding at Barrow, jute at Dundee, straw hats at Luton, boots and shoes at Northampton, cutlery at Sheffield, was not seriously misrepresenting the facts. In the nine-teenth century, it was generally thought right that each district should concentrate on producing what it could turn out best and cheapest; the negligible cost of transport would see to it that the most economical product would knock out its competitors for a very long distance around. Diversification of industry, to spread the risk of slumps, was a twentieth-century palliative.

Correspondingly, the countryside began to empty, with a kind of draught-board pattern by which the countrymen nearest the towns moved into them, those in the next squares farther out took their places, and their own were taken by people from still farther away. Oversea migration was of course a different kind of thing altogether. As the steel ribbon of railway advanced the frontier westwards over the American prairies between 1870 and 1900, men from every country in Europe accompanied it; and the European railways and steamship lines worked together to move many thousands of emigrants from every European land to the Atlantic and across it.

That was an age of economic upheaval. When did this dynamic force finally expend itself? In its classic, nineteenth-century form, based on coal, steam, and steel, the end came in 1914. From that date, military necessity forced forward the development of the internal-combustion engine which emerged in the 1920s as a revolutionary of a new order, on land and in the air. But there was a difference between the railway revolution and the motor-engine revolution. The railway had no competitor on land, in terms of technical efficiency, except for a very few transport tasks of minor and local importance, which the horse-drawn vehicle still performed. The internal-combustion engine on the road could not, and still cannot, perform a considerable range of work with efficiency equal to the railway's. This explains why most of the governments of the world are at this time encouraging railways to 'modernize' their equipment, with diesel or electric traction, and why new railways are being built in many parts of the world – Russia, Yugoslavia, China, central Africa, Queensland – where the primary stage of modern economic development (the 'colonial' stage, in a non-political sense) is only now being begun.

There are certain functions, then, for which the railway has not been superseded as the most effective means of transport on land. At the lower end of the scale of distance, the road motor vehicle has such advantages of flexibility and economy with small loads that it can establish itself against the railway both for passengers and, perhaps with even greater success, for goods. At the upper end, the aircraft by its speed, once it is in the air, can abstract very much of the longer-distance passenger traffic, especially where the railway route involves awkward features like ship or train-ferry connexions, and it can even take away some small proportion of the highest-value long-distance freight traffic. The great question for the railwayman, and the airman, of the future is the shortest distance at which the air will be able to compete effectively with the rail. The answer, it seems, will depend mainly on developments with helicopters or aircraft with some other form of vertical take-off. It remains at the moment to be seen whether such machines can be made big enough to carry loads which really pay, taking all costs into account, and how far the problems of navigating above large cities and landing in their centres can be overcome.

It is probably very foolish to attempt any guess at the future, at a time when technological changes of vast import will certainly be introduced within the next decade; but it had better be faced. It may be hazarded that in countries where there is a well-developed road system the railway has a more than fair chance of maintaining its position as the principal haulage agency of passengers on main routes for distances between 25 and 200 miles – perhaps up to 300 miles, as railway speeds are improved and air travel becomes more unattractive. This will mean not only new rolling stock and signalling; between certain of the greatest traffic centres completely new routes will have to be constructed.

In densely crowded urban and suburban areas the figure of 25 miles can be reduced to 5, or even 3, miles because the roads are so seriously congested. For haulage of freight, there is no maximum distance – the longer the haul, the better placed the railway is to deal with it at an economic charge; but the lower limit of distance may be considerably above the 25 miles we have given for passengers. For most goods, railways may find it difficult to retain their business at distances below 100–150 miles, except when they are dispatched regularly in considerable density between the same points, justifying special terminal equipment and perhaps even specialized rolling stock.

'Justifying special equipment' – this is the essence of the whole railway matter. The railway is a complex of specialized equipment which must be fairly fully utilized to produce an economic result. Its strength, as well as its weakness, is summed up in the name of its basic component, the 'permanent way'. What is permanent is also necessarily rather rigid. The rigidity of the railway enables it to carry large loads at good speeds, with safety; but it makes it unadaptable. Yet any survey, however brief, of the history of railways in their 130 years of life so far must bring out one lesson above all: successful railways have welcomed change, not resisted it indefinitely. In transport, as in most other things, change and development are the essence of life; and railways at this time have to face more fundamental changes than ever before. In particular, they have to face and accept the most unwelcome change of all, which is the need to relinquish the attempt to perform tasks that can now be done better by other agencies. They must deliberately shed the small, awkward, unremunerative jobs that never did pay very well, if at all, but were accepted by older generations of railwaymen, and of the public, as part of their general duty.

The railway's obligation to carry every load that is offered to it is something that has become very firmly fixed in the thinking of railwaymen and of the public. It arose naturally in the conditions of near-monopoly that the railways once enjoyed; tradition and a decent anxiety to meet all kinds of social needs make many railwaymen unhappy about giving up any of the services they have been rendering for many years. For similar reasons, some sections of the public feel that they have a right to railway services that are demonstrably uneconomic, taken by themselves; it is even claimed that the railway should be there ready to provide service when the alternative on the road or in the air is overloaded or temporarily not available. Unless there is a massive support from public funds, after a deliberate political decision that the railway is to be supported as a matter of social policy, the railways cannot play this role and live.

On the passenger side, it is already possible to prepare development plans which take account of the traffics that ought clearly to be shed and of those that, with skill and enterprise, can reasonably be expected to be retained. But on the freight side, the picture of the future is much less clear. Serviceable estimates of the volume of passenger travel ten years and more ahead can be produced; but it is impossible to do anything of the sort for the basic freight traffics. How much coal and steel will be produced in any country in 1970? And how much of that production will be transported by rail? And how far? New techniques for pipelining and for transmission of electric current, for example, may considerably reduce the volume of long hauls for the heavy freight traffics which most railways rely on, and the balance of their freight and passenger haulage may be completely altered. This is the great question for the railways' future.

But there is no need to conclude with a question mark. Against these uncertainties, a number of positive statements can be set down about the way in which the railway can overcome its inherent disadvantages of rigidity and specialization and utilize to the full its inherent advantages of high capacity and dependability. The potential for sustained speed is the railway's greatest asset. But to develop this potential, many features of present-day railway operation which inhibit the full exercise of speed must be removed. If movement along the rails is to be secured at a more constant, and higher, speed, all trains must be able to start and stop at approximately the same rate and maintain the same top speed. This means that the present great difference between passenger and freight train speeds must be removed, which can be achieved only when freight trains are fitted with continuous brakes (and are composed of vehicles having the same stability at high speeds). When they can be pulled up in the same distance as an express passenger train, then they can be permitted to run at express passenger speeds. Constant speed between stops also implies that differences in the character of trains – express, 'semi-fast', and stopping – which work over the same tracks become less tolerable, and the train making odd intermediate stops will be recognized as something that hinders the attainment of the line's potential capacity. Certainly the number of 'lineside' stopping stations on long-distance main lines, outside suburban areas, is likely to decrease very greatly.

If the railways are to make the best of their potential capacity for haulage between terminal points, it will be important to take particular trouble about what happens at the terminals themselves. Transhipment must be made as easy and convenient as possible, both for passengers, by means of improved interchange to onward distribution facilities by road, and for freight. In the freight field, particular opportunities exist for reducing handling by the use of containers, pallets, 'piggy-back' transport (road to rail and back to road again), and the like. The business of shunting, that is, breaking up trains and recoupling the vehicles into fresh trains, is wasteful and will have to be reduced far below present levels. The ideal is to run 'block trains' regularly to and fro without breaking up the train formation and remarshalling it. This ideal is unattainable in full on most railways; but it is perfectly feasible to run trains much more to a pattern, and to cut down shunting. Equipment (especially freight wagons) must be standardized, not only nationally but internationally, so that the fullest use can be made of it in service; 'common user' must be universal, so that no wagon is hauled empty where it could be carrying a load. With standard equipment, also, maintenance costs can be reduced by reducing the number of spare parts that must be held.

Up to the present time, schemes of railway modernization have been essentially local – that is, national rather than international in their inspiration and execution. Loading gauges, braking systems, signals, methods of electrification vary from country to country in Europe, and technical solutions of great ingenuity (and often high cost) have been devised to overcome the difficulties created by the technicians them-selves. Standardization across national borders has not been achieved – often it has not even been attempted. In Africa, as well as in Europe, it is already evident how much this divergence of practices is frustrating the full economic use of the railways; if real freedom of exchange is to be ensured, the railways will have to standardize themselves.

A programme of the kind indicated in the preceding pages may sound, when thus abstractly set out, quite sensible and straightforward; but in practice it will prove, if it is faithfully followed through, to call for great courage and tenacity in those responsible for its achievement. The principles will constantly be called into question by the travelling public, traders, disinterested critics, politicians, competitors, and by some railwaymen themselves; and particular applications of the principles are certain to arouse great local and sectional hostility. But if it is carried through, a new railway system will be created which will serve the community well. There will be a new railway age; and this generation will not be able to answer one of the questions that we began with: 'When did it end?'

[Completed 1962]

Postscript, 1998

That is where this essay of the 1960s left off – with a string of questions. In the interval, few of them have been answered. Leaving the text as a 'period piece', without alterations prompted by hindsight, I round off this reissue with some reflections on developments in the British transport scene as it appears now.

After 1914, and even more after 1945, the transport scene began to change, and to change fast: the original railway age had gone, and new forms of transport, on the road and in the air, had arrived and marched ahead. These were bound to make such an impact on the railways' traffics that new responses, indeed a whole new habit of thought and practice, were evidently necessary, though it was not evident to many people for some time. In Britain, the railways were often criticized, as they always have been, for sluggishness and resistance to change in thinking and practice; yet the kinds of response that I foresaw as required were already being adopted in the 1960s and have since been carried forward. Within individual countries, that is: it still remains true that 'standardization across national borders has not been achieved'. Even with the long-delayed completion of the Channel Tunnel in 1994, linking Britain and the continent of Europe with a railway line providing through running for passenger and freight vehicles, and with the reduction of formalities at the frontiers of countries within the European Community, that is still the case. There have been adjustments for the benefit of through working – train crews do not now always have to be changed at national borders; but in essence the national networks are still there, with some modifications of local practices to remove the most tiresome forms of diversity in operation. But there is still no standard automatic coupler for all rolling stock throughout the whole of Europe. However, to try to attempt a survey of world-wide developments in the last thirty-five years would require another book, and another author; this postscript limits itself to offering some consideration of the situation of railways in Britain.

Here there has been ceaseless argument about the future of the railways: technical, commercial, and political. By 1997 a new organization was in place, consisting essentially of an 'infrastructure' company (Railtrack), owning and maintaining track, structures, and signalling, and a number of operating companies to which sections of the system are 'franchised' for specific periods. It is hoped that this arrangement, which includes a formidable array of checks and balances, will result in the public and the economy being better served by commercially keen entrepreneurs than they were by the allegedly hidebound managements of the former regime. The process itelf has been expensive, and 'public relations' gimmickry has not been lacking – the public has been invited to believe that train services will be improved if the rolling stock is painted in different colours. But this is hardly the main issue: good marketing there must be, but this is useful only if the product is felt to be worth buying. The main issue, rarely mentioned in the huge quantity of writing about the railways' future, is: Will there be an adequate flow of new capital into the railway business? Devices like disposing of surplus properties can be used, once (like 'selling off the family silver'); but there is little more of that left to sell, and in the long run there must be continuous and assured capital investment. Under total control by the State, this was never assured; it was never even contemplated. A railway, like any other activity with a large technical content (such as engineering plants, or hospitals, or motorway networks), must not stop capital spending at any point; if it does, it does not stay still but it goes backwards, in relation to its customers and its competitors. So the great unsolved (indeed, usually unasked) question is: Will enough capital be found? And, very much in the mind of the potential capitalist: Will it be remunerated?

A flow of surplus income, sufficient to remunerate the capital invested after all expenses have been paid, can be secured in different ways: by earning enough in receipts from the business itself (the traditional way); or by securing guaranteed subvention from the State or other public bodies to make up a shortfall; or by association, as a permanent partner, in a diversified group of businesses which values the railway element and will support it from its general revenues – much as the old railways retained subsidiary loss-making activities like some canals, docks, and hotels for their value to the undertaking as a whole. Occasional individual sections of railway line in unusual situations may show a profit, in the ordinary commercial sense; but it is unlikely that, however skilfully managed, any complete systems of railway networks will ever do so again. Support from public funds, a hand-to-mouth expedient dependent on politics, is not a stable foundation on which to build and maintain a railway system which must be constantly evolving and improving. The third course, association with wider industrial groups, seems to offer the best chances for soundly-based development. Whether the vertical division between the providers of infrastructure and the train operators is sensible and will prove lasting looks doubtful; and the allocation of lines to particular operators seems certain to undergo changes. We may be at the start of a renewed onset of railway imperialism – not by means of construction this time, but by absorption and amalgamation.

Experience in the world of transport since the 1960s has shown, in Britain and in most developed countries, growth in two fields that was not indeed unexpected, though the actual volumes of increase were hardly foreseen: air transport and road transport. Unrestrained by fears of noise, pollution, and congestion, the facility for greatly increased mobility offered by the aircraft and the road vehicle has proved irresistible. The proliferation of air traffic has produced serious problems of congestion, not only in the air itself but even more at and surrounding the airports; on the roads, the motor car and the lorry, bestowing on individuals and communities a hitherto unsuspected range of choice and amenity, swamp the highways and the towns, so much that when a new relief road is opened a host of new problems immediately arise; for the motor car abhors a vacuum, and the new space is quickly filled.

In all this, where does the railway stand? On the freight side, I wrote above: 'For most goods, railways may find it difficult to retain business at distances below 100–150 miles', except in some special cases. In the ensuing years, the bottom has dropped out of the railway freight market, so that in 1994–5 only 97.4 million tonnes were carried against 228.54 million tons in 1965. Except for a few limited traffics, freight now moves by road within Britain.

So what is left for the railways in the way of passenger business? I guessed in 1962 that 'in countries where there is a well developed road system the railway has a more than fair chance of maintaining its position as the principal haulage agency of passengers on main routes for distances between 25 and 200 miles. In densely crowded urban and suburban areas the lower figure can be reduced to 5, or even 3, miles because the roads are so seriously congested.'

In these thirty-five years little has happened in the way of technical development to require this forecast to be altered. In one particular area, this issue has been clearly perceived and some action taken. The dream of city centre airports served by aircraft which take off and land vertically remains unfulfilled; and wherever the airport is, the landward transport remains a thorny problem. Cleveland, Ohio, was the first large city to serve its airport by an extension of its urban railway system (1968); London Heathrow was the world's first capital city airport to have an underground railway link (1977); the other London airports, Gatwick and Stansted, are served by main-line trains, and so are Birmingham and Manchester. Airport-to-city movement has been recognized as demanding railway transport; but the lesson goes further than that. For big cities with large concentrations of population, the railway, in some form, is accepted to be an indispensable link in the throughout journey, performing in a way that no airborne or road-based vehicle can be expected to do, and is an essential component in their internal communications.

The future for the railway, whatever its particular technical form (orthodox main line, underground, or in some hybrid form like an updated tram, now fashionably called LRT – light rapid transit, though it is not particularly light in weight), must lie in the making of sensible decisions about where its real strength lies and in concentrating effort in that area. This may sound a bleak doctrine to those who cherish the country branch-line, a freight service to and from everywhere, cross-country connections between places of minor importance (except to the few enthusiasts); but nostalgia is no sound basis for business decision. Those railway managements will prevail and survive which decide firmly what kinds of business they are best at handling, and manage to secure adequate capital to keep the services they offer fully up to date and felt by the users to be reliable. Second only to safety, reliability is above all what the public expects from railways. It is much better, if not very glamorous, to perform what you have undertaken to do rather than promise something more exciting and fall short from time to time. An assured journey time of 2 hours 10 minutes is better than a promise of 1 hour 55 minutes which is not achieved by 20 per cent of the trains. Provided that the railways can carry on, day in day out, a service that is safe and reliable, there is an important place for them: not the one that they filled in the railway age, but one that developed communities, living in high densities, of the next age will find that they cannot do without. It will be better for them to decide that now, rather than wait for more painful experience to convince them that it is true.

Notes on sources

Place of publication is London unless specified otherwise.

Chapter 1 (pages 5 to 10)

C. E. Lee, *The Evolution of Railways* (2nd ed., 1943), is the basic study of its subject; the definition quoted here is on p. 104. For the Parliamentary fence, E. S. Fay, 'Fencing the Railway: Then and Now', *British Transport Review* 4 (1957), p. 235; receipts from passengers and freight, 1843–52, H. G. Lewin, *The Railway Mania and its Aftermath* (1936), p. 114; the Leeds & Selby, G. C. Dickinson, 'Stage-Coach Services in the West Riding of Yorkshire between 1830 and 1840', *Journal of Transport History* 4 (1960), p. 1, and W. W. Tomlinson, *The North Eastern Railway* (Newcastle [1915], p. 260); public control, D. S. Landes, *The Unbound Prometheus* (Cambridge, 1969), quotation from p. 399; C. F. Adams, *Railroads: Their Origin and Problems* (revised ed., New York, 1876), p. 80.

Chapter 2 (pages 11 to 14)

C. F. D. Marshall, *History of British Railways down to the Year 1830* (Oxford, 1938) is a general account that must be used with caution; much more information has since come to light and been published in different places. For the north-eastern wagon ways, Marshall, plate 10 (map of 1812); C. E. Lee, 'The World's Oldest Railway', *Transactions of the Newcomen Society* 25 (1947), p. 141; 'Tyneside Tramroads of Northumberland', *ibid.* 26 (1949), p. 199; 'The Wagonways of Tyneside', *Archaeologia Aeliana*, 4th ser., 29 (1951), p. 135; eighteenth-century wagon way accounts, E. Hughes, *North Country Life in the Eighteenth-Century: the North-East, 1700–50* (Oxford, 1952), ch. v, especially pp. 153–8. For archaeology of the subject, M. J. T. Lewis, *Early Wooden Railways* (1970), esp. p. 51 and pl. 26; B. Baxter, *Stone Blocks and Iron Rails* (1966). The date for the Wollaton Hall line, given by Marshall and Lee as 1598, is more likely

1603–4 (R. S. Smith, 'Huntingdon Beaumont: Adventurer in Coalmines', *Renaissance and Modern Studies* I (1957), p. 115). On the Stockton & Darlington, W. W. Tomlinson, *The North Eastern Railway* (Newcastle, [1915]); J. S. Jeans, *Jubilee of the World's First Public Railway* (1875); *Rail 150*, ed. J. Simmons (1975), especially ch. 1, pp. 13–46, by K. Hoole; P. J. Holmes, *The Stockton & Darlington Railway 1825–1975* (Ayr, [1975]); M. W. Kirby, *The Origins of Railway Enterprise* (Cambridge, 1993). On the Liverpool & Manchester, R. E. Carlson, *The Liverpool & Manchester Railway Project 1821–1831* (1969); T. J. Donaghy, *Liverpool & Manchester Railway Operations 1831–1845* (1972); R. H. G. Thomas, *The Liverpool & Manchester Railway* (1980); on the events of the opening day, J. C. Jeaffreson, *Life of Robert Stephenson* (1864), 1, 157–64, based on eye-witness account by T. L. Gooch.

Chapter 3 (pages 15 to 22)

On George and Robert Stephenson, the classic life is by Samuel Smiles in his *Lives of the Engineers* (1st ed., 1857, G. Stephenson only, later editions revised); the only satisfactory modern treatment at full length is L. T. C. Rolt, *George and Robert Stephenson* (1960); a short study, M. Robbins, *George and Robert Stephenson* (1966, rev. ed. 1981). For Telford's organization, L. T. C. Rolt, *Thomas Telford* (1958); proceedings on the 1825 L. & M. R. Bill, F. S. Williams, *Our Iron Roads* (1st ed., 1852), appendix A; track gauge, C. E. Lee, 'Some Railway Facts and Fallacies', *Transactions of the Newcomen Society*, 33 (1960), p. 1; the Bolton & Leigh letter, J. Simmons, 'Railway History in English Local Records', *Journal of Transport History* I (1954), pp. 167–8. 'Standard' biographies, which have their defects, are: J. C. Jeaffreson, *Life of Robert Stephenson* (2 vols, 1864); I. Brunel, *Life of Isambard Kingdom Brunel* (1870); J. Devey, *Life of Joseph Locke* (1862); A. Helps, *Life and Labours of Mr. Brassey* (1872); O. J. Vignoles, *Life of Charles Blacker Vignoles* (1889). More modern lives are: C. B. Noble, *The Brunels: Father and Son* (1938); L. T. C. Rolt, *Isambard Kingdom Brunel* (1957); N. W. Webster, *Joseph Locke: Railway Revolutionary* (1970); C. Walker, *Thomas Brassey: Railway Builder* (1969); K. H. Vignoles, *Charles Blacker Vignoles: Romantic Engineer* (Cambridge, 1982). Sidelights on the engineers of the early period are thrown by an anonymously-published work, *Personal Recollections of English Engineers* (1868), written by F. R. Conder (reprinted as *The Men who Built Railways*, ed. J. Simmons (1983)), and *John Brunton's Book*, ed. J. H. Clapham (Cambridge, 1939).

Chapter 4 (pages 23 to 29)

The physical development of the British railway system is well summarised in the relevant chapters of Sir John Clapham's great work, *An Economic History of Modern Britain* (3 vols, Cambridge, 1926–38); they are vol. 1, ch. ix; vol. 2, ch. v (with a map of the railway system in 1872); and vol. 3, ch. vi. Greater detail can be found in C. E. R. Sherrington, *Economics of Rail Transport in Great Britain* (1928), vol. i, and in the same author's *Hundred Years of Inland Transport* (1934). C. H. Ellis, *British Railway History* (2 vols, 1954 and 1959), is a popular account. J. Simmons, *The Railways of Britain* (1961), ch. i, has a good summary; ch. viii is an excellent guide to the literature and maps existing at that date. See also H. Perkin, *The Age of the Railway* (1970); H. Pollins, *Britain's Railways* (1971); H. J. Dyos and D. H. Aldcroft, *British Transport* (1969).

For a comprehensive survey, see *The Oxford Companion to British Railway History*, ed. J. Simmons and G. Biddle (Oxford, 1997).

There are many books and publications on the history of individual railway companies, and of branch lines, and even of stations. These are listed and indexed (up to 1983) in G. Ottley, *Bibliography of British Railways*, 1(2nd ed.) (1983); vol. 2 (supplement, 1988), contains addenda to that date: a valuable compilation. Histories of some of the larger companies that I have found most useful, from the point of view of this essay, have been: W. W. Tomlinson, *The North Eastern Railway: Its Rise and Development* (Newcastle, [1915]); E. T. MacDermot, *History of the Great Western Railway* (2 vols, 3 parts, 1927 and 1931); C. F. D. Marshall, *History of the Southern Railway* (2nd ed., 1963; 1st ed. unreliable); G. Dow, *Great Central* (3 vols, 1959–65); J. Wrottesley, *The Great Northern Railway* (3 vols, 1979–81); J. Marshall, *The Lancashire & Yorkshire Railway* (3 vols, 1969–72); R. A. Williams, *The London & South Western Railway* (3 vols, 1968–88, vol. 3, on the twentieth century, with J. N. Faulkner); M. C. Reed, *The London & North Western Railway* (Penryn, 1996). On early railways in Scotland, C. J. A. Robertson, *The Origins of the Scottish Railway System 1772–1844* (Edinburgh, 1983).

The series *Regional History of the Railways of Great Britain*, by different authors (15 vols, 1960–89), full of chronological detail, aims also to indicate the railways' impact on the life of the communities in the areas covered. The books are of varying merit; the best perhaps D. S. M. Barrie on South Wales (1980).

Jack Simmons's works, *The Railway in England and Wales 1830–1914* (Leicester, 1978), *The Railway in Town and Country 1830–1914* (Newton Abbot, 1986), and *The Victorian Railway* (1991), are unequalled in the breadth of their range of inquiry and reference to economic and social life.

For railways in 1850, with tabulations, maps, and much careful detail, H. G. Lewin, *The Railway Mania and its Aftermath, 1845–1852* (1936); P. Bagwell, *The Railway Clearing House in the British Economy 1842–1922* (1968). My rough calculations on the consumption of iron and timber are based on indications given by Tomlinson, *N. E. R.*, pp. 405–6, Clapham, vol. 1, pp. 425–8, and D. Lardner, *Railway Economy* (1850), p. 48. Contemporary accounts of George Hudson appear in J. Francis, *History of the English Railway* (2 vols, 1851), and D. Morier Evans, *Facts, Failures, and Frauds* (1859); R. S. Lambert wrote a life, *The Railway King* (1934); more recent lives by A. J. Peacock (2 vols, York, 1988–9), and B. Bailey (Stroud, 1995).

Labour Party pamphlets of 1945 (*Railways for the Nation*) and 1955 (*British Transport*); Lord Stamp's remark, W. V. Wood and J. Stamp, *Railways* (1928), p. 12; the story about Lord Petre is in Francis's *History*, 1, pp. 256–9. On Charles Austin, see *Dictionary of National Biography*; Bedfordshire landowners, F. S. Williams, *The Midland Railway: Its Rise and Progress* [1876], p. 139.

Chapter 5 (pages 30 to 33)

For a detailed study of a country branch, H. W. Parris, 'Northallerton to Hawes: a Study in Branch-Line History', *Journal of Transport History* 2 (1956), p. 235; C. L. Mowat, *The Golden Valley Railway* (Cardiff, 1964), quotation from p. ix; contractors' lines, H. Pollins, 'Railway Contractors and the Finance of Railway Development in Britain', *Journal of Transport History* 3 (1958), pp. 41, 103; competition, P. S. Bagwell, 'The Rivalry and Working Union of the South Eastern and London, Chatham & Dover Railways', *Journal of Transport History* 2 (1956), p. 65. For general comment on the railways in this period, W. Ashworth, *An Economic History of England 1870–1939* (1960), pp. 109–26.

Chapter 6 (pages 34 to 46)

Sydney Smith's letter, *Works of the Rev. Sydney Smith* (1845), iii, pp. 427–8; *The Times*, 12 January 1850, 20 October 1851, 30 October 1838 (quoting *Birmingham Advertiser*); fish traffic, *Railway Times*, 3 June 1848; newspapers, *History of The Times*, 11 (1939), pp. 83, 347; G. P. Neele, *Railway Reminiscences* (1904), p. 205; G. Dow, *Great Central* ii (1962), p. 340; telegraphs, J. H. Clapham, *Economic History of Modern Britain* i (1926), pp 395–6, quoting D. Lardner, *Electric Telegraph Popularized* (1855), p. 273; mail pick-up apparatus, *Railway Gazette* supplement, 'The First Main-Line Railway', 16 September 1938, p. 47; Cavour,

M. Walker (ed.), *Plombières* (New York, 1968), p. 45; the companies' schools, P. W. Kingsford, 'Labour relations on the Railways, 1835–1875', *Journal of Transport History* 1 (1954), p. 71; the Strome Ferry affair, *British Railways Magazine* (Scottish Region), January 1950, p. 11; D. Brooke, 'The Opposition to Sunday Rail Services in North-Eastern England', *Journal of Transport History* 6 (1963), p. 95; the Anti-Sunday Travel Union, *Surrey Comet*, 20 June 1889; *Railway Magazine* 24 (1909), pp. 512–13; *Brighton Herald*, 20 July 1889; local time, *Railway Gazette*, Great Western Railway centenary supplement, 30 August 1935, p. 7; the watch, V. S. Haram, *Centenary of the Irish Mail* (1948), p. 31; A. Prentice, *Historical Sketches and Personal Recollections of Manchester* (1851); J. R. Kellett, *The Impact of Railways on Victorian Cities* (1969); C. E. Lee, *Passenger Class Distinctions* (1946); Allport on the M. S. & L., O. J. Vignoles, *Life of C. B. Vignoles* (1889), p. 229; A. J. C. Hare, ed. M. Barnes, *The Years with Mother* (1952), p. 33; the merchant princes, *Official Guide to the L. B. S. C. R.* (8th ed., 1912), p. 28; G. O. Clayton, 'Club Trains of the L. M. S.', *Locomotion* 7 (1936), pp. 21, 33; excursions, R. Marchant, 'Early Excursion Trains', *Railway Magazine* 100 (1954), p. 426; R. E. Carlson, *The Liverpool & Manchester Railway Project 1821–1831* (1969), p. 235; R. A. Williams, *The London & South Western Railway* i (1968), p. 103; *The Times*, 26 August 1840; Cook's, W. F. Rae, *The Business of Travel* (1891), and J. Pudney, *The Thomas Cook Story* (1953); temperance at Camborne, *British Railways Magazine* (Western Region), August 1952, p. 154; the York & North Midland opening, R. S. Lambert, *The Railway King* (1934), pp. 46–9; the Fat Ox, *Great Western Railway Magazine*, January 1934, p. 27; the Paignton pudding riot, J. T. White, *History of Torquay* (1878), pp. 231–3.

On early railway travel by royalty, E. T. MacDermot, *History of the Great Western Railway* i (1927), pp. 659–66, and three chapters containing much curious detail in G. P. Neele, *Railway Reminiscences* (1904), pp. 447–531. For journey times to Devonshire, C. Torr, *Small Talk at Wreyland* (abridged ed., 1926), pp 206–9; J. H. Newman, *Apologia pro Vita Sua* (1948 ed.), Note A, p. 199; G. M. Young, *Victorian England: Portrait of an Age* (1936), p. 7; 'railroad speed', *The Times*, 5 November 1840, quoted by J. Wake, *The Brudenells of Deene* (1953), p. 375; the Excursion Train Galop cover, C. B. Andrews, *The Railway Age* (1937), pl. 14; Northampton, J. Wake, *Northampton Vindicated* (1935); Uxbridge, M. Robbins, *Middlesex* (1953), p. 78, and *Points and Signals* (1967), p. 103; Kingston, R. W. C. Richardson, *Surbiton* (1888), pp. 9–10; H. W. Hart, 'The Late Development of the Railway Facilities of Kingston-upon-Thames', *Journal of the Railway & Canal Historical Society* 13 (1967), p. 2; Sedbergh, *Manchester Guardian*, 25 September 1953.

Chapter 7 (pages 47 to 56)

W. Wordsworth, sonnet 'On the Projected Kendal and Windermere Railway', *Works*, ed. E. de Selincourt and H. Darbishire, iii (1946), p. 61; *Works of John Ruskin*, ed. E. T. Cook and A. Wedderburn, xxvii (1907), p. 86; opposition to railways on grounds of amenity, W. T. Jackman, *Development of Transportation in Modern England*, ii (Cambridge, 1916), pp. 497–500; J. C Jeaffreson, *Life of Robert Stephenson*, i (1864), pp. 268-70; 'Lord Harborough's curve', C. E. Stretton, *History of the Midland Railway* (1901), pp. 81–6, and J. Simmons in *Victoria History of Leicestershire*, iii (1955), p. 118; house at Idsworth, N. Pevsner and D. Lloyd, *Hampshire and the Isle of Wight* (Buildings of England, 1967), p. 305; T. R. Potter, *History and Antiquities of Charnwood Forest* (1842), p. 187; [R. J. King], *Murray's Handbook for Travellers in Surrey, Hampshire, and the Isle of Wight* (2nd ed., 1865), p. 37; *George Eliot's Life, Letters, and Journals*, ed. J. W. Cross (new ed. [1887]), p. 37; English scenery before the railways, W. G. Hoskins, *The Making of the English Landscape* (1955), pp. 154–7, 187–9. For a gazetteer of surviving monuments of railway architecture and engineering, G. Biddle and O. S. Nock, *The Railway Heritage of Britain* (1983).

For railway architecture generally, C. Barman, *Introduction to Railway Architecture* (1950); C. L. V. Meeks, *The Railway Station* (1957); M. Kubinsky, *Bahnhöfe Europas* (Stuttgart, 1969); D. Cole, 'Mocatta's Stations for the Brighton Railway', *Journal of Transport History* 3 (1958), p. 149; H. Parris, 'British Transport Historical Records and their Value to the Architectural Historian', *Architectural History* 2 (1959), p. 50; Lime Street, C. F. D. Marshall, *Centenary History of the Liverpool & Manchester Railway* (1930), p. 71; early criticism of extravagance, F. Whishaw, *The Railways of Great Britain and Ireland* (1840), p. 281 (London & Croydon), p. 320 (Manchester & Leeds), pp. 364–5 (Northern & Eastern), pp. 367–8 (North Midland); Cubitt's King's Cross, *Builder* 9 (1851), p. 731; Currey on London Bridge, *Builder* 20 (1862), p. 163; horrors beyond the Tees, W. W. Tomlinson, *North Eastern Railway* [1915], pp. 412–14; Moreton-on-Lugg, *Railway Magazine* 11 (1902), pp. 65–6 (there is a picture of this quaint object in the collection at Dunster Castle, Somerset); Cardiff (Queen Street), E. L. Ahrons, *Locomotive and Train Working in the latter Part of the Nineteenth Century*, iv (1953), p. 91; A. Trollope, *The Belton Estate* (World's Classics ed.), p. 81; for splendid photographs, F. W. Houghton and W. H. Foster, *Story of the Settle-Carlisle Line* (Bradford, 1948).

Chapter 8 (pages 57 to 64)

For 1851 statistics, quoted from Board of Trade reports, F. S. Williams, *Our Iron Roads* (1852 ed.), pp. 274–5; allowance has to be made to exclude the Irish proportion from the totals. Recruitment from agricultural labourers, C. Torr, *Small Talk at Wreyland* (1970 ed.), first part, p. 45. For the alleged continuity of employment from canal-building, A. Helps, *Life and Labours of Mr. Brassey* (1872), p. 76; S. Smiles, *Lives of George and Robert Stephenson* (1874 ed.), p. 250, said that men from the Fen districts of Lincoln and Cambridge formed the cadre; R. Lloyd, *Railwaymen's Gallery* (1953), p. 34; Woodhead tunnel, G. Dow, *Great Central* i (1959), ch. v; J. Simmons, 'The Building of the Woodhead Tunnel', *Parish and Empire* (1952), p. 155; R. A. Lewis, 'Edwin Chadwick and the Railway Labourers', *Economic History Review* 3 (1950), no. 1; Mickleton tunnel, E. T. MacDermot, *History of the Great Western Railway* i (1927), pp. 494–6; the chaplain's evidence, Select Committee on Railway Labourers, *Report* (1846), Q. 2528, quoted by Clapham, i, p. 412; H. Cresswell, *Winchmore Hill: Memories of a lost Village* (2nd ed., 1912), p. 111; T. Coleman, *The Railway Navvies* (1965); D. Brooke, *The Railway Navvy* (1983). Coachmen, R. A. Williams, *The London & South Western Railway* i (1968), p. 227; G. J. Turnbull, 'A Note on the Supply of Staff for the Early Railways', *Transport History* 1 (1968), p. 3; the Weatherburns, 'Veritas Vincit', *Railway Locomotive Management* (Birmingham, 1847), pp. 23, 30 (with list of all the original Liverpool & Manchester drivers); C. E. Stretton, *History of the Midland Railway* (1901), p. 20; C. R. Clinker, 'The Leicester & Swannington Railway', *Transactions of the Leicestershire Archaeological Society* 30 (1954), p. 99; *Railway Magazine* 18 (1906), p. 199; J. C. Jeaffreson, *Life of Robert Stephenson* (1864), ii, p. 266; R. H. G. Thomas, *London's First Railway – the London & Greenwich* (1972), p. 102; on Edmondson, W. W. Tomlinson, *The North Eastern Railway* (Newcastle, [1915]), pp. 421–2; J. S. MacLean, *The Newcastle & Carlisle Railway* (Newcastle, 1948), pp. 114–15; J. B. Edmondson, *Early History of the Railway Ticket* (1878, reprint 1968); P. Bagwell, *The Railway Clearing House* (1968), pp. 37–8; L. Wiener, *Passenger Tickets* [1939]. On Crewe, W. H. Chaloner, *Social and Economic Development of Crewe* (Manchester, 1950); B. Reed, *Crewe Locomotive Works and its Men* (1982); Wolverton, F. E. Hyde and S. F. Markham, *History of Stony Stratford* (1948); *Victoria History of Buckinghamshire*, ii (1908), pp. 126–7; Swindon, H. B. Wells in L. V. Grinsell and others, *Studies in the History of Swindon* (1950), pp. 93–160; D. E. C. Eversley in *Victoria History of Wiltshire*, iv (1959), pp. 207–19; K. Hudson, 'Early Years of the Railway Community in

Swindon', *Transport History* 1 (1968), pp. 130–52; J. Cattell and K. Falconer, *Swindon: the Legacy of a Railway Town* (1995); generally, B. J. Turton, 'The Railway Town', *Town Planning Review* 32 (1961), pp. 97–115, and 'The Railway Towns of Southern England', *Transport History* 2 (1969), pp. 105–35.

Great Western uniforms, MacDermot, *G. W. R.*, pp. 669–76; wage rates in the forties, 'Veritas Vincit' (cited above) and M. Robbins, 'The North Midland Railway and its Enginemen, 1842–3', *Points and Signals* (1967), pp. 132–9; P. W. Kingsford, 'Labour Relations on the Railways, 1853–1875', *Journal of Transport History* 1 (1954), p. 65, with list of strikes, and *Victorian Railwaymen: the Emergence and Growth of Railway Labour 1830–1870* (1970); P. S. Bagwell, 'Early Attempts at National Organization of the Railwaymen', *Journal of Transport History* 3 (1958), p. 94; P. W. Kingsford, 'The Railway Clerk in 1851', *Transport Salaried Staff Journal,* September and October 1951, pp. 386, 423; G. W. Alcock, *Fifty Years of Railway Trade Unionism* (1922); G. D. H. Cole and R. P. Arnot, *Trade Unionism on the Railways* (1917); P. S. Bagwell, *The Railwaymen* [N.U.R.], 2 vols, 1963, 1982.

Chapter 9 (pages 65 to 75)

'The Passing of the Railway Director', *Railway Gazette*, 26 December 1947; G. Alderman, *The Railway Interest* (1973); J. Elliot, 'Early Days of the Southern Railway', *Journal of Transport History* 4 (1960), p. 107; G. P. Neele, *Railway Reminiscences* (1904), pp. 284, 378; on Sir Lowthian Bell, R. Bell, *Twenty-Five Years of the North Eastern Railway* [1951], p. 7; early complaints correspondence, [G. R. Smith] *Old Euston* (1938), pp. 39–58; development of organization, M. R. Bonavia, *Economics of Transport* (1936), pp. 73–5; M. Robbins, 'General Managers', *Points and Signals* (1967), pp. 147–60; G. Findlay, *The Working and Management of an English Railway* (5th ed., 1894), pp. 1–36 (biographical sketch by S. M. Phillp); T. R. Gourvish, *Mark Huish and the London & North Western* (1972); the events of 1888–94, Clapham, ii, pp. 196–8, iii, pp. 355–62; G. Alderman, *The Railway Interest* (1973), pp. 108–28, 144–60; P. Cain, 'Traders versus Railways', *Journal of Transport History* n. s. 2 (1973), p. 65; MacDermot, *G. W. R.*, ii, ch. ix, 'Prosperity and Repose'; Sir Richard Moon, Neele, pp. 377–9, and M. C. Reed, *The London & North Western Railway* (1996); alleged preferential rates, W. M. Acworth, *The Railways and the Traders* (1891), pp. 9–16.

The story of brakes, H. Ellis, *Nineteenth Century Railway Carriages* (1949), pp. 56–9; state intervention, H. Parris, *Government and the Railways in Nineteenth-Century Britain* (1965); opposition to the block telegraph, Sir Daniel

Gooch's letter to the Board of Trade in 1872, qu. in MacDermot, ii, pp. 87–9; the Canonbury accident and Mr. Christison, Neele, pp. 289–92; absolute block working, MacDermot, *G. W. R.*, ii, pp. 302–3; C. F. D. Marshall, *History of the Southern Railway* (1936), pp. 470–1; posters, Neele, p. 215, stockholders, Bonavia, pp. 57–9; free tickets, M. Robbins, *Railway Magazine* 113 (1967), p. 470, 114 (1968), p. 451, 115 (1969), p. 43; Mr. Seneca Hughes, C. H. Grinling, *History of the Great Northern Railway* (1898), pp. 81, 172.

Chapter 10 (pages 76 to 90)

The Stockton & Darlington Railway, W. W. Tomlinson, *The North Eastern Railway* (Newcastle [1915]), pp. 69, 85, 46n.; *Diaries of Edward Pease*, ed. A. E. Pease (1907); J. S. Jeans, *Jubilee Memorial of the Railway System: a History of the Stockton & Darlington Railway* (1875), esp. pp. 293, 296; H. Pollins, 'Aspects of Railway Accounting before 1868', *Studies in the History of Accounting*, ed. A. C. Littleton and B. S. Yamey (1956), p. 332; 'Railway Auditing: a Report of 1867', *Accounting Research* 8 (1957), p. 14; 'The Marketing of Railway Shares in the First Half of the Nineteenth Century', *Economic History Review* 7 (1954), p. 230; 'The Finances of the Liverpool & Manchester Railway', *Economic History Review* 5 (1952), p. 90; *The Times*, 30 September 1850; Stovin, R. A. Williams, *The London & South Western Railway*, i (1968), pp. 219–20; M. Robbins, 'The Redpath Frauds on the Great Northern Railway', *Points and Signals* (1967), p. 139; R. B. Fellows, *The Canterbury & Whitstable Railway* (1930), pp. 28, 75–8; MacDermot, *G. W. R.*, i, 19–21; J. Butt and J. T. Ward, 'Promotion of the Caledonian Railway Company', *Transport History* 3 (1970), p. 243; D. Brooke, 'Promotion of four Yorkshire Railways and the Share Capital Market', *Transport History* 5 (1972), p. 264; S. A. Broadbridge, 'Sources of Railway Share Capital', *Railways in the Victorian Economy*, ed. M. C. Reed (1969), p. 184 (the Lancashire & Yorkshire Railway, rather a special case); M. C. Reed, 'Railways and the Growth of the Capital Market', *ibid.*, p. 162.

For contractors, H. Pollins, 'Railway Contractors and the Finance of Railway Development in Britain', *Journal of Transport History* 3 (1958), pp. 41, 103; the Liverpool & Manchester dividend, W. T. Jackman, *Development of Transportation in Modern England*, ii (Cambridge, 1916), pp. 529–31. For railway earnings, see tables of dividends in *Bradshaw's Shareholder's Guide and Railway Manual* (annual); C. E. R. Sherrington, *Economics of Rail Transport in Great Britain* (1928), ii, pp. 32–3; W. M. Acworth, *Elements of Railway Economics* (1905), pp. 15–16. On state ownership, Lord Londonderry, quoted in Clapham, i, p. 414; see also i, pp. 417–18, ii, pp. 188–90; E. Cleveland-Stevens, *English Railways: Their Development and their Relation to the State* (1915); W. A. Robertson, *Combination among Railway Companies* (1912); E. E. Barry, *Nationalisation in British Politics* (1965), ch. 3, esp. pp. 96–7; Churchill, speech at Glasgow, 11 October 1906; Parliamentary committee hearings, C. H. Grinling, *History of the Great Northern Railway* (1898), *passim*. On the scrap at Chester, MacDermot, *G. W. R.*, i, pp. 356–7, at Wolverhampton, *ibid.* i, pp. 372–5; at Manchester, Grinling, *G. N. R.*, pp. 163–4; at Nottingham, *ibid.*, p. 121. On social distinctions, *Murray's Handbook for Lancashire* (new ed., 1880), p. xxvi.

Chapter 11 (pages 91 to 101)

The literature of world railways is enormous. The following notes give references only to books that have been consulted; many figures have been taken from periodicals, mainly from the *Railway Gazette*. A useful outline table, by decades, of railway mileage development throughout the world appeared in *The Railway Handbook* (last published 1947–8, pp. 52–3). The most up-to-date information can usually be found in *Jane's World Railways*, issued annually. Many articles on historical development of railways overseas have appeared in the *Railway Magazine* since 1897, to which there is unfortunately no cumulative index; for European railways, there has usually been an article in the centenary year.

For *Locomotion*, F. T. Schultze, *Die Ludwigsbahn: die erste deutsche Eisenbahn* (Leipzig, 1935), p. 41; Buenos Aires, M. Robbins, 'The Balaklava Railway', *Points and Signals* (1967), p. 177; Vauxhall in Russia, *Railway Gazette*, 18 November 1949; *Lady Charlotte Guest: Extracts from her Journals*, ed. Lord Bessborough (1950), pp. 45, 141–2, 153, 157, 161; J. G. H. Warren, *Century of Locomotive Building* (1923), pp. 93–4 (R. Stephenson & Co.); A. Helps, *Life and Labours of Mr. Brassey* (1872), map opp. p. 52; Haswell, *Railway Magazine* 95 (1949), p. 52; Hughes, *Manchester Guardian*, 28 May 1953; British engineering influence in Europe, W. O. Henderson, *Britain and Industrial Europe, 1750–1870* (Manchester, 1954); capital movements, A. K. Cairncross, *Home and Foreign Investment 1870–1913* (1953), pp. 1, 2, 8; T. Veblen, *Imperial Germany and the Industrial Revolution* (1915; Ann Arbor, 1966 ed.), p. 130; H. Adams, *The Education of Henry Adams* (1919), p. 43.

For Ireland, H. G. Lewin, *Early British Railways 1801–1844* [1925] and *The Railway Mania and its Aftermath 1845–1852* (1936); J. C. Conroy, *History of Railways in Ireland* (1928); K. A. Murray, *Ireland's First Railway* [Dublin & Kingstown] (Dublin, 1981); E. M. Patterson, *The Great Northern Railway of*

Ireland (Lingfield, 1962); K. A. Murray and D. B. McNeill, *The Great Southern & Western Railway* (Dublin, 1971); E. Shepherd, *The Midland Great Western Railway of Ireland* (Leicester, 1994); L. M. Cullen, *Economic History of Ireland since 1660* (1972), pp. 142–4, 152–3, 168–9. For India, J. N. Sahni, *Indian Railways: One Hundred Years* (New Delhi, 1953); J. N. Westwood, *Railways in India* (1974); M. Satow and K. Desmond, *Railways of the Raj* (1980); M. B. K. Malik, *Hundred Years of Pakistan Railways* (Karachi, 1962). For Australia, [L. I. Paddison] T*he Railways of New South Wales, 1855–1955* (Sydney 1955); E. Harding, *Uniform Railway Gauge* (Melbourne, 1958); on New Zealand gauges, A. W. Palmer and W. W. Stewart, *Cavalcade of New Zealand Locomotives* (Auckland and Wellington, rev. ed., 1965); R. S. Fletcher, *Single Track: the Construction of the North Island Main Trunk Railway* (Auckland, 1978). For Africa, *The South African Railways: History, Scope, and Organization* (Johannesburg, 1947); *A Century of Transport 1860–1960* (Johannesburg, 1960); L. van Onselen, *Head of Steel* (Cape Town, 1962); E. D. Campbell, *Birth and Development of the Natal Railways* (Pietermaritzburg, 1951); M. F. Hill, *Permanent Way*, i (Kenya and Uganda) (Nairobi [1951]), ii (Tanganyika) (Nairobi [1959]); R. Hill, *Sudan Transport* (1965); L. Wiener, *L'Egypte et ses Chemins de Fer* (Brussels, 1932).

Chapter 12 (pages 102 to 114)

M. Robbins, 'Hitler's Broad-gauge Railway', *Journal of Transport History*, 3rd ser., 4, no. 1 (1983), p. 67, reviewing A. Joachimsthaler, *Die Breitspurbahn Hitlers* (Freiburg, 1981); J. H. Clapham, *Economic Development of France and Germany 1815–1914* (4th ed., Cambridge, 1936); A. L. Dunham, *Industrial Revolution in France 1815–48* (New York, 1955); P. Dauzet, *Le Siècle des chemins de Fer en France* (1821–1938) (Fontenay-aux-Roses, 1948); L.-M. Jouffroy, *L'Ere du Rail* (Paris, 1953); *Histoire des Chemins de Fer en France*, pref. L. Armand (Paris, 1963); on Belgium, D. Lardner, *Railway Economy* (1850), ch. xviii; U. Lamalle, *Histoire des Chemins de Fer Belges* (Brussels, 1953); A. Linters (ed.), *Spoorwegen in Belgie* (Gent, 1985); Netherlands, G. Hupkes, *Treinen* (Amsterdam, 1964); Germany, *Hundert Jahre deutsche Eisenbahnen* (Berlin, 1935); B. Stumpf, *Geschichte der deutsche Eisenbahnen* (Mainz/Heidelberg, 1960); *Zug der Zeit: Zeit der Züge: Deutsche Eisenbahn 1835–1985*, ed. M. Jehle and F. Sonnenberger (Nuremberg, 1985); R. Fremdling, *Eisenbahnen und deutsche Wirtschaftswachstum 1840–1879* (Dortmund, 1985); W. Klee, *Preussische Eisenbahngeschichte* (Stuttgart, 1982); A. Mühl and K. Seidel, *Die württembergischen Staatseisenbahnen* (Stuttgart, 1970); Goethe's conversation with Eckermann, 23 October 1828; Treitschke, qu. in

Clapham, *France and Germany* (above), p. 150; Denmark, *Danmarks Jernbaner*, ed. M. Buch and C. I. Gomard, vol. 1 (history) (1933, reprinted Roskilde, 1987); Switzerland, *Railways of Switzerland* (*Railway Gazette*, 1947); E. Mathys, *Beiträge zur schweizerischen Eisenbahngeschichte* (Berne, 2nd ed., 1954) and *Männer der Schiene* (Berne, 2nd ed., 1955); *Bahn Saga Schweiz*, ed. H. P. Treichler (Zurich, 1996); Cavour's article, M. Walker, *Plombières* (New York, 1968), pp. 46–62 (uncut original text in D. Zanichelli (ed.), *Gli Scritti del Conte di Cavour* (Bologna, 1892), ii, pp. 3–50); F. Tajani, *Storia delle Ferrovie Italiane* (Milan, 1939); F. Ogliari and P. Muscolino, *1839–1989: Centocinquant' Anni di Trasporti in Italia* (Milan, 1989); *Railways in Spain, 1848–1958* (Madrid, 1958); F. Wais, *Historia de los Ferrocarriles Españoles* (2nd ed., Madrid, 1974); *Die österreichischen Eisenbahnen, 1837–1937* (Vienna, 1937); *100 Jahre Semmeringbahn* (Vienna, 1954); J. N. Westwood, *History of Russian Railways* (1964); P. E. Garbutt, *Russian Railways* (1949); H. Maier, *Die erste russische Eisenbahn: von Sankt Petersburg nach Zarsko Selo und Pawlowsk* (Berlin, n.d., c.1988); M. Alameri, *Eisenbahnen in Finnland* (Vienna, 1979); F. Stöckl, *Eisenbahnen in Südosteuropa* (Vienna, 1975).

Chapter 13 (Pages 115 to 121)

For United States railroads generally, C. F. Adams, Jr., *Railroads: Their Origin and Problems* (new ed, New York, 1876); E. A. Pratt, *American Railways* (1903); F. H. Spearman, *The Strategy of Great Railroads* (New York and London, 1905); S. Thompson, *Short History of American Railways* (New York and London, 1925); S. H. Holbrook, *Story of American Railroads* (New York, 1947); J. F. Stover, *American Railroads* (Chicago, 1961) and *The Life and Decline of the American Railroad* (New York, 1970) – Isaac Dripps, p. 20; G. R. Taylor and I. D. Neu, *The American Railroad Network, 1861–1890* (Harvard, 1956); J. F. Stover, *Railroads of the South, 1865–1900* (Chapel Hill, N.C., 1955); the Civil War books cited under notes on ch. 14; for the iron and steel figures, D. L. Burn, *Economic History of Steelmaking, 1867-1939* (Cambridge, 1940), pp. 18, 19, 28, 73; for Canada, N. Thompson and J. H. Edgar, *Canadian Railway Development from the Earliest Times* (Toronto, 1933); G. P. de T. Glazebrook, *History of Transportation in Canada* (Toronto, ed. 2, 1964); G. R. Stevens, *Canadian National Railways* (2 vols, Toronto, 1960, 1962); J. L. McDougall, *Canadian Pacific* (Montreal, 1968).

For Dickens's comments, *American Notes* (first published 1842; New Oxford Illustrated ed., 1957), pp. 62–4, 113–15, 153; for Trollope's, *North America* (ed. 5, 1866), pp. 36, 71, 136, 140, etc.; W. M. Acworth, *The Railways and the Traders* (1891), pp. 1, 5.

Chapter 14 (pages to 122 to 135)

For this chapter generally, E. A. Pratt, *Rise of Rail Power in War and Conquest* (Philadelphia and London, 1916), with good bibliography. London & Birmingham bill, 'The Struggle to obtain Parliamentary Powers for the Building of the London & Birmingham Railway Line', *Journal of the Stephenson Locomotive Society* 41 (1965), p. 318; London & Southampton bill, S. Fay, *A Royal Road* (Kingston, 1883), pp. 16–17; *Quarterly Review* quoted by J. Francis, *History of the English Railway* (1851), i, pp. 102–3; use of canal, *The Times*, 19 December 1806; F. C. Mather, 'The Railways, the Electric Telegraph, and Public Order during the Chartist Period 1837–48', *History* 38 (1953), p. 40; armoured trains and the circular railway, W. B. Adams, *Roads and Rails* (1862) and letter, *The Times*, 28 July 1859: M. Robbins, 'William Bridges Adams and his "Roads and Rails"', *Points and Signals* (1967), p. 56; Launceston branch, M. Robbins, 'Railways and Politics in East Cornwall', *ibid.*, p. 74; Mestre-Vicenza, G. M. Trevelyan, *Manin and the Venetian Revolution of 1848* (1923), pp. 133, 179; the Crimea, M. Robbins, 'The Balaklava Railway', *Points and Signals* (1967), p. 163; B. Cooke, *The Grand Crimean Central Railway* (Knutsford, 1990); the Andrews raid, quoted from R. C. Black III, *Railroads of the Confederacy* (Chapel Hill, N.C., 1952, pp. 143–4; R. S. Feuerlicht, *Andrews' Raiders* (New York, 1963); G. E. Turner, *Victory rode the Rails* (Indianapolis and New York, 1953); T. Weber, *Northern Railroads in the Civil War, 1861–1865* (Columbia, 1952). On Menelik E. Mathys, art. on Alfred Ilg, *Männer der Schiene* (Berne, 2nd ed., 1955), p. 65; F. Jacqmin, *Les Chemins de Fer pendant la Guerre de 1870–1871* (Paris,, 2nd ed., 1874); Baron Ernouf, *Histoire de Chemins de fer Français pendant la Guerre Franco–Prussienne, 1870–71* (Paris, 1874, reprinted 1980); M. Howard, *The Franco-Prussian War* (1961); E. W. C. Sandes, *The Royal Engineers in Egypt and the Sudan* (Chatham, 1937); L. A. C. Raphael, *The Cape to Cairo Dream* (Columbia, 1936); E. P. C. Girouard, *History of the Railways during the War in South Africa, 1899–1902* (1903); P. E. Garbutt, 'The Trans-Siberian Railway', *Journal of Transport History* 1 (1954), p. 238; S. G. Marks, *Road to Power: the Trans-Siberian Railroad and the Colonization of Asian Russia 1850–1917* (1991); M. Jastrow, Jr., *The War and the Bagdad Railway* (Philadelphia and London, 1917); H. Pönicke, *Die Hedschas- und Bagdadbahn* (Düsseldorf, 1958); S. Khairallah, *Railways in the Middle East: Political and Economic Background* (Beirut, 1991). For 1914–18, A. M. Henniker, *Transportation on the Western Front* (British Official History of the Great War, 1937), introduction by J. E. Edmonds; M. Peschaud, *Les Chemins de Fer pendant la Guerre 1914–1918* (*Revue Générale des*

Chemins de Fer et des Tramways, Paris, 1919); A. Sarter, *Die deutsche Eisenbahnen im Kriege* (Stuttgart and Yale, 1930); for 1939–45, C. I. Savage, *Inland Transport* (History of the Second World War, 1957); P. Durand, *La S.N.C.F. pendant la Guerre: sa Résistance à l'Occupant* (Paris, 1968); E. Kreidler, *Die Eisenbahnen im Machtbereich der Achsenmächte während des Zweiten Weltkrieges* (Frankfurt, 1975); A. S. Kliomin and others, *Militärtransporte Richtung Front* (East Berlin, 1986); for U. S. Military Railway Service, C. R. Gray, Jr., *Railroading in Eighteen Countries* (New York, 1955); 'Victory is the … flower', W. S. Churchill, *The River War* (1960 ed.), p. 157 and all ch. viii.

Index